Henry Seddall

The missionary History of Sierra Leone

Henry Seddall

The missionary History of Sierra Leone

ISBN/EAN: 9783743317130

Manufactured in Europe, USA, Canada, Australia, Japa

Cover: Foto ©ninafisch / pixelio.de

Manufactured and distributed by brebook publishing software
(www.brebook.com)

Henry Seddall

The missionary History of Sierra Leone

THE MISSIONARY HISTORY
OF
SIERRA LEONE.

BY THE

REV. HENRY SEDDALL, B.A.,

TRINITY COLLEGE, DUBLIN.
RECTOR OF FORGNEY, CO. LONGFORD.
AUTHOR OF "MALTA: PAST AND PRESENT."

"If the Church, in any of its branches, is not making converts by home and foreign missions, it is not in that place answering the purpose for which it was instituted."—*Dean Hook's Life of Archbishop Parker.*

LONDON:
HATCHARDS, 187 PICCADILLY.
1874.

PREFACE.

During the five years that it was my privilege to labour as Deputation Secretary of the Church Missionary Society in Ireland, I was frequently asked whether there existed any book in which a complete, and yet concise account of the Society's labours amongst the heathen was given. I was obliged to reply that no such book existed; that, in fact, the history of the Society's work was scattered through a large number of books, tracts, pamphlets, and periodicals, inaccessible to many persons who feel a real interest in missionary work.

I have endeavoured in the following pages to supply the want that undoubtedly exists. Whether I have succeeded in doing so, it will be for those who read what I have written to say.

Sierra Leone being the first field that was occupied by the Church Missionary Society, it occurred to me that it might be well to give some account of the wonderful work that has been done there, before proceeding to describe the results of labour in other parts of the mission field.

I lay no claim to originality. I have merely related in my own words what I gathered from other books; and have quoted the words of other authors where it seemed advisable to do so. I have tried to be accurate, without being prolix, and concise without being obscure; and I have also aimed at relating events in the order in which they actually occurred.

"The Missionary History of Sierra Leone," as narrated in the following pages, only takes account of what has been done by the Church Missionary Society in that colony. Not that I ignore the labours of other Societies, or refuse to acknowledge that much of the good effected in Sierra Leone is due to those labours; but that I possess little or no information concerning the operations of other Societies, and am therefore not qualified to write about them; and also that this little book is intended chiefly for the use of those who are members of the Church Missionary Society, and are anxious to help on its work. I may add that whilst I acknowledge most readily the zeal, the energy, the perseverance, and the piety of the missionaries who are connected with the Protestant dissenting churches, I feel a very decided preference for the doctrine and discipline of the church of which I am a minister, and a desire that the missionary success of that church may be as widely known as possible. And after all, those who know Sierra Leone must admit that the Church Missionary Society has borne "the burden and the heat of the day" in that colony; and that the present prosperous condition of its inhabitants is due *mainly*, if not exclusively, to the ardent zeal, the manly self-denial, and the fervent piety of missionaries of the Church of England, sent out by the Society.

The Wesleyan missionaries, following in the steps of their brethren, the church clergy, catechists, and schoolmasters, have with them nobly contended in West Africa against error, and have fought valiantly for the truth. The existence of forty graves in the burial ground at Sierra Leone, containing the bodies of as many missionaries, or missionaries' wives, fully attests their deep devotion to the cause of Christ; but even these Wesleyan missionaries themselves, would confess if questioned, that the van in the fight which has been carried on by this "noble army of martyrs" has always been occupied by the sons and daughters of the Church of England. Every Christian ought to know something about the missionary history of, at least, that branch of the Church of Christ of which he is a member.

This little book may, with God's blessing, be the means of communicating some knowledge of missionary work and kindling some zeal for it. If it produce this result, I trust I may at some future time be enabled to relate what great victories have been gained over heathenism in other countries—in India, in China and Japan, in New Zealand, and North West America.

I send it forth with the earnest prayer that it may prove useful to those for whom it is specially intended; and that it may serve to create an interest in the great and glorious work which has been done, and which, with the help of God, is now being done amongst the heathen by the Church Missionary Society.

The following Books and Papers were carefully consulted in the preparation of the following narrative: viz.—

THE WHITE MAN'S GRAVE: a Visit to Sierra Leone in 1834. By F. H. RANKIN.

A RESIDENCE AT SIERRA LEONE. By a Lady; Edited by the HON. MRS. NORTON.

MISSIONS IN WESTERN AFRICA. By the REV. S. A. WALKER, M.A.

- CHURCH MISSIONS IN SIERRA LEONE. By the same Author.
- MEMOIR OF THE REV. EDWARD BICKERSTETH. By the REV. T. R. BIRKS.
- MEMOIR OF THE REV. JOSIAH PRATT, B.D. By his Sons.
- REPORTS OF THE DIRECTORS OF THE AFRICAN INSTITUTION from 1814 to 1823.
- CHURCH MISSIONARY INTELLIGENCER from 1849 to the present time.
- CHURCH MISSIONARY RECORD.
- CHURCH MISSIONARY GLEANER.
- CHURCH MISSIONARY QUARTERLY AND OCCASIONAL PAPERS.
- FROM POLE TO POLE.
- THE AFRICAN SLAVE TRADE AND ITS REMEDY. By SIR T. F. BUXTON, M.P.
- MEMOIR OF REV. W. A. B. JOHNSON.
- THE NIGER EXPEDITION: Journals of REV. J. F. SCHÖN and MR. S. CROWTHER.
- THE CHRISTIAN TRAVELLER.
- CHURCH MISSIONARY PAMPHLET ON THE SIERRA LEONE MISSION.
- THE AFRICAN SLAVE BOY: a Memoir of the RIGHT REV. SAMUEL CROWTHER, D.D., Revised by himself.
- THE ANNUAL REPORTS OF THE CHURCH MISSIONARY SOCIETY.
- NEWSPAPERS AND PAMPHLETS published at Sierra Leone.

CONTENTS.

CHAP.		PAGE.
I.	Sierra Leone: its Climate and its Inhabitants	1
II.	The War against Slavery	24
III.	The Pioneers	52
IV.	First Drops of the Shower of Blessing	77
V.	The Leaders of the Forlorn Hope	107
VI.	Onward Still	138
VII.	The Niger Expedition	166
VIII.	Africa's Black Bishop	192
IX.	The Victory of Faith	214

THE MISSIONARY HISTORY OF SIERRA LEONE.

CHAPTER I.

SIERRA LEONE: ITS CLIMATE AND ITS INHABITANTS.

> "Wild tornadoes
> Strewing yonder sea with wrecks;
> Wasting towns, plantations, meadows;
> Are the voice with which He speaks."
>
> . . . . .
>
> "Skins may differ, but affection
> Dwells in white and black the same."—COWPER.

SIERRA LEONE is a peninsula on the Western coast of Africa, about 26 miles long and 12 broad. It contains an area of 300 square miles. The shore is low; but rugged mountains rise in the interior to the height of 3000 feet. The serrated outline of these mountains suggested the name which it bears. It was known to the Portuguese as early as the year 1442, and was even then employed by them and by other nations as a convenient spot for carrying on the negro slave trade. The Spanish name Sierra Leone, that is the "mountain of lions," was originally applied to the range of mountains which form the chief body of the peninsula now designated by that name. In Spanish and Portuguese, as in Latin, the literal meaning of Sierra (serra) is *saw;* and the term as applied to a chain of mountains, indicates their rugged outline, which presents an appearance not unlike the teeth of a saw.

Sierra Leone labours under a singularly bad reputation; and he who for the first time bids farewell to his European home and friends, to reside for a time in that colony, shares, to a very great extent, the feelings of the soldier who leads a forlorn hope against an enemy's fortress.

The northern frontier of the peninsula stretches from Cape Sierra Leone in lat. 8° 30′ N.; long. 13° 43′ W., to the river Bunce, which marks its eastern boundary. The ocean washes its coast from the Cape to the southern point at Kate's river, between which and the Bunce four or five miles only of land intervene. Its outline, therefore, nearly forms a triangle, two sides of which consist of mountains and valleys, green with the never-fading verdure of jungle and forest. Sierra Leone first attracted the attention of the people of Great Britain in 1563, when Admiral Sir John Hawkins landing there, made unsparing use of fire and sword, and after perpetrating every atrocity that his depraved nature could suggest, captured some hundreds of the natives, put them on board his vessels, and afterwards sold them as slaves for his own advantage. It was at a much later period, however, that England coveted its admirable situation and rich resources, and determined to colonise it.

The face of the peninsula is now studded with towns and villages. The inhabitants of many of them are liberated slaves, who have been rescued from cruel bondage and distributed through the several districts of the colony. Freetown, the capital, is considerable in extent and contains a large population. It is the seat of government, and the centre from which commercial operations are carried on. It stands on the northern shore, about five miles from Cape Sierra Leone. At this point the arm of the sea, which is fifteen miles in width between the Cape and Leopard's Island, narrows to six or seven miles. To the left the shore is broken into a series of little bays, with hills gently rising above and waving with palm trees. In front is the river glittering in constant sunshine, and bordered by the low woods of the Bullom shore. The inland country to the west is intersected by the waters of Port Logo, the Rokel, and the Bunce rivers, varied with many a green island, and bearing many a little canoe, formed of the trunk of a tree and paddled by sturdy negroes. The aspect of the country immediately behind Freetown is bold and imposing; it is a succession of evergreen mountains soaring one above the other. No site more lovely for a town could have been selected. The town itself is picturesque. It rises from the water's edge and gradually creeps up the sides of the surrounding hills, with its white dwellings and prolific gardens, whilst in the distance, emerging from high woods, appear the country mansions of gentlemen, with patches of ground surrounding them, which are devoted to the production of coffee and fruits. The style in which the houses are generally built gives an Oriental air to the landscape. Most of them stand in a court-yard or garden, causing the extent of space covered by buildings to be much greater than in an European town of equal population; and giving it, from the foliage of luxuriant trees, a healthy and fresh appearance.

On nearing the land after a voyage from England of about three weeks in a steamer, or about six weeks in a sailing vessel, you first trace the distant mountains indistinctly, and can hardly discern whether they are mountains or clouds; but on approaching them more closely, you see them stand before you in quiet majesty, clad from top to base in the mantle of a rich tropical *flora* of variegated green. Instead of meadows and crops of corn like those which we are accustomed to at home, you will see on the sides of the mountains the cassada plantations, which are to the poorer classes of negroes what potatoes are to the Irish peasant; and where the ground does not admit of cultivation, you will find it covered with a rough kind of reed grass, so high that the grazing cattle are completely hidden by it. The tops of the mountains are covered with a wild and almost impenetrable thicket of forest, the abode of monkeys, gazelles, leopards, and other beasts; but the base of the mountains, directly above the level of the sea, is adorned with a beautiful garland of lofty palm trees, the slender leafless stems of which are surmounted by a large tuft of long feathered leaves or branches, which looks down from its dazzling height, the very picture of serene calmness and peaceful security. It is directly under this crown of branches that the useful palm-nuts grow in large clusters, which afford the well-known palm oil so largely employed in the manufacture of soap and candles in Europe, so serviceable for greasing the axles of railway carriages, and so profitable to the negroes by amply supplying to them the want of butter and lard. Besides these palms there are many other trees which at once characterise the country as a tropical one. There are the large-leaved banana and plaintain trees, almost drawn down to the ground by the weight of their own enormous clusters of fruit; the apocator tree, concealing its huge pears amid the dark green leaves with which it is decked; there also appears the rich foliage of the mango tree, interspersed with its innumerable yellow fruits of a peculiar turpentine taste; and high above all rises the gigantic cotton tree, covered all over with a mail of long sharp spikes, and year after year dropping its silky cotton, to be scattered about by the busy activity of the land and sea breezes. The whole of the vegetation around you has a new and tropical appearance, and convinces you at every glance that you have arrived in a distant and sunny land.

But the romantic scenery, the brilliant sky, and the glorious green of the trees and shrubs, are more than counterbalanced by the fever which slays its hundreds, the storms which strike terror into the heart of the bravest, and the every-day annoyances arising from myriads of reptiles, and millions of insects. There are few whom the fever does not attack; and many whom it attacks it kills. Until the British settler in Sierra Leone has been two or three times laid prostrate by the fever, and has fought his way, with the help of God, through each successive attack, he can hardly feel sure of his continued existence from day to day. After recovering from two or three attacks, he may consider himself "seasoned" or "acclimatized."

The storms of Sierra Leone can hardly be realized by those who have not witnessed them. They defy description. "The bare remembrance of the tornado," says the author of "Letters from Sierra Leone," "leads me to think the unhealthiness of the climate, and all the lesser discomforts attendant on living in so outlandish and uncivilized a place as Sierra Leone, nothing in comparison to the horror of these tropical storms that now make me tremble, though at first I used to watch their progress with admiration."

The earliest tornadoes generally take place in April, exhibiting an awfully grand phenomenon of nature. After having observed the eastern horizon illuminated every evening, for perhaps a whole fortnight, with streaks of lightning, and hearing now and then the sound of distant thunder in the direction of the continent approaching nearer, and growing louder every day, all at once, on a calm and oppressively hot afternoon, a cloud may be seen rising in the east, and gradually spreading over the sky, presenting a well-defined straight line across the hemisphere as it nears the zenith. The declining sun in the west continues to cast his rays on these massive piles of overhanging clouds, as if to show them up in their deepest shade of blackness, and to render their appearance in the highest degree formidable. Whilst all are now looking in dread anticipation on these fire-charged vapour-masses towering one above another, and having nearly reached the zenith, the death-like stillness is suddenly broken by a tremendous blast of wind rushing forth from the clouds, and raging with such fury for several minutes, that it is scarcely possible for any man to stand against it. On this a vivid flash of lightning darts through the air, immediately followed by a crashing peal of thunder, and by the heavy fall of large drops of rain. Now the tornado has regularly set in; the clouds have extended themselves over the whole heavens, pouring down such torrents of rain as to darken the atmosphere. This twilight darkness is momentarily lighted up by brilliant flashes of lightning, following each other in rapid succession, and forcing their zigzag course in all directions. A sulphureous smell pervades the air, and not unfrequently fireballs which are emitted from the clouds, may be seen bursting and falling to the ground. Simultaneous roars and claps of thunder, which shake the houses to their very foundations, keep up a deafening concert, re-echoing over land and sea. This wild tumult of nature, in which heaven, and earth, and sea, seem to mingle, and in which fire, and storm, and water, threaten to be equally destructive, generally does not last longer than about half-an-hour, after which it passes on to the sea, and disappears in the western horizon. The close and heavy atmosphere which, before the tornado, seemed to lie on everyone's limbs like a nightmare, is now purified, and has become light and clear, and a complete calm directly succeeds the most frightful roar of the elements, so that one can hardly realize how, an hour before, this noiseless calm and benign sunshine should all have been preceded by such a dread disturbance.

Amongst the "lesser discomforts" mentioned above, may be reckoned the reptiles and insects. Night, instead of being the friend of the weary, is his deadliest foe in Sierra Leone; instead of bringing with it "tired nature's sweet restorer, balmy sleep," it calls in an army of enemies, who array themselves in deadly hostility to the sleeper. The enormous cockroach crawls over his body, and, if permitted, nibbles the ends of his fingers, producing a wound difficult to cure. The prying mantis, a fat, green, loathsome insect, sometimes produces blindness by attacking the eye with its crab-like claws. Mosquitoes, the offspring of pestilential marshes, swarm in countless numbers, and one single mosquito in a bed-room is sufficient to destroy all hope of repose. Small amber ants, which infest every house, spread themselves at night over the sleeper's bed; large tarantulas fall upon him from the ceiling; gigantic black crickets ingeniously perch themselves near his ear in some hidden nook, whence they "grate harsh music." If all these living and noxious creatures be not sufficient to disturb his slumbers, the prickly heat plunges beneath the white man's skin, and stings him with ten thousand stings, making him rush from his couch in sheer despair, and bitterly rue the day when he landed on the sun-lit shores of Sierra Leone.

Let us see, now, who are the inhabitants of Sierra Leone.

They may be divided into two great classes, *Colonists* and *Liberated Slaves*.

The Colonists are of five classes :—
1. The Settlers.
2. The Maroons.
3. Foulahs and Mandingoes.
4. Kroomen.
5. Europeans.

Each of these classes must be considered separately.

SETTLERS. The Settlers are the descendants of the free blacks who, before the outbreak of the American War of the last century, had been the proprietors of cultivated land in the Southern States of America. Throughout the whole of the contest between the States and England, these blacks remained loyal to the latter country; and therefore, when the war was brought to a close, and the States were declared independent of the mother country, they lost all their property by fines and by plunder. The English Government, in order to compensate them for their losses, assigned them residences and lands in Nova Scotia, but the climate proved too cold for their constitutions, accustomed to the sunny South, and the knowledge of agriculture which they had gained in Carolina and Virginia, was useless to them in the northern latitudes to which they had been transferred. A mercantile company which had purchased a belt of land on the northern shore of Sierra Leone, therefore, offered to convey these unhappy negroes from Nova Scotia to this African home, where the climate was suited to their constitutions, and where the soil was similar to that of their forfeited American estates. The free grant promised consisted of twenty acres of land for each man, ten for his wife, and five for each child. Tempted by the many inducements held out to them, upwards of eleven hundred embarked at Nova Scotia, and settled at Sierra Leone. Further particulars of this migration will be given in the next chapter.

MAROONS. The word Maroon is supposed to be a corruption of a Spanish word signifying marauder or plunderer. Some, however, think that it is merely a mis-pronunciation of the word *Moor*, whom the Maroons resemble in complexion. They had their origin in Jamaica, from an intermixture of several white and black races, when, during the early connection of the Spaniards with that island, runaway slaves not unfrequently secured their liberty in the impenetrable forests. The Maroon is, by descent, European, American, and African; and he combines in his person the vices, with very few of the virtues, of these three races.

Whilst the Spaniards held Jamaica, the independence of the Maroons was acknowledged; and the English, on capturing the island, confirmed their privileges. Not long after the English occupation of Jamaica, a rebellion broke out, in which the most dreadful atrocities were perpetrated by the Maroons. The rebellion having been suppressed, the inhabitants of the revolted district, together with their chiefs, were sent to Nova Scotia, and subsequently, in the year 1800, to Sierra Leone, on the occasion of a disturbance among the Settlers there.

At Sierra Leone they assisted the English to quell the disturbance which had arisen amongst the colonists; and thus they brought on themselves an amount of hatred which shows itself, not unfrequently, even at the present time. Five hundred and fifty Maroons landed at Sierra Leone in 1800, and they have ever since been increasing in numbers, and acquiring considerable wealth. As merchants and storekeepers, many of them have amassed large fortunes, and have been able to give their sons the benefit of a good education in England; whilst the less wealthy members of the community have contrived to earn, as labourers and mechanics, a decent and respectable livelihood. The Maroons, as a race, profess no form of religion. Many of them, however, have joined the Wesleyan Methodist body.

FOULAHS AND MANDINGOES. Amongst the various tribes who have settled at Sierra Leone, the Foulahs and Mandingoes are remarkable in their appearance and mode of life. They are Mohammedans. The Foulahs belong to several distinct nations. Some live on the banks of the Senegal; others on the confines of the kingdom of Bournoo; others at Timbuctoo or Soudan. In the extensive territory lying between the Senegambia and Guinea, are the Foulahs of Guinea. Representatives of all these tribes or nations are to be found in Sierra Leone.

The Foulah arrests attention by his strong Arab and occasionally Roman features, the long ringlets that hang down to his shoulders, his thoughtful eye, his measured step, and his rosary of beads generally carried in his hand. You cannot mistake him. He is a disciple of the Prophet of Mecca. He is the gold merchant of the coast, and he is more than suspected of being a slave merchant too. It is important to bear in mind that the proper Foulahs are not of the negro race, nor are they the original inhabitants of the countries in which they live. Their features are European. Their hair is straight and silky, and their skin of a tawny hue, inclining to copper. These proper Foulahs, are, however, less numerous than the black Foulahs, who have sprung from the intermarriages of this tawny race with the negroes. This is the reason why Foulahs are sometimes mentioned in books on Africa as black men and at other times as red men.

There are, in fact, two distinct kinds or classes of Foulahs. In the Foulah suburbs of the capital of Sierra Leone, may be seen artisans diligently employed in working at various trades; making sandals and pouches, plaiting straw for hats, or writing verses out of the Koran for sale. Silver rings of very large dimensions, shield-shaped, and stamped with abstruse hieroglyphics, are favourite specimens of their art. In steel and leather work, the Foulahs excel. Africa has long been celebrated for its leather. The Foulahs prepare it in a superior manner, giving it substance and suppleness. In appearance and smell it resembles Russian leather. The woods are rich in barks which contain the astringent substance used by the tanner; and from the same source are procured plants of various kinds, which impart to the tanned leather many rich and brilliant colours.*

The Mandingoes are easily distinguished from the Foulahs by their complexion. Some of them are remarkably tall and very black. They are generally well made. They are described as a very gentle race; cheerful in their dispositions, inquisitive,

* The Mandingoes come from the kingdom of the same name near the sources of the Niger, extending eastward through Bambara and westward to Bambrook and Woolly. The name Mandingo, however, seems to denote rather conversion to the tenets of Mohammed than connexion with any tribe or nation. The Mandingoes of Sierra Leone are chiefly Soosoos or Timmanees who have exchanged the worship of the devil for the tenets of the Koran.

simple, credulous, and fond of flattery. But they are at the same time very passionate, and their quarrels often end in bloodshed. All who have written on the subject of Sierra Leone agree in saying that the Foulahs and Mandingoes are the greatest knaves in the colony. They labour under the suspicion of kidnapping the free blacks of Sierra Leone and transferring them to the opposite Bullom shore. The author of "A Residence at Sierra Leone," describes them as great hunters, and says that "when they sit down to cook the game they have killed at a large fire kindled for that purpose on the hill side, their tall figures, with the gaudy caps, flowing upper garments, bare legs, and sandalled feet, flitting before the flames in the dusk of the evening and handling their long formidable-looking muskets, present quite a picture, that reminds you in its wildness of some of Salvator Rosa's."

The same writer says:—"On the breaking up of some of their fasts they present an imposing spectacle as they assemble in one dense crowd upon the grass field near their own quarter, each dressed in his robe of state, seated on a white sheep skin, and holding a red, green, or yellow umbrella over his head, the wealthiest of them galloping on to the field on their spirited Foulah horses as if advancing to the charge at the head of a regiment ; the women decked out in the gayest of scarf head-dresses, with the children seating themselves at some distance on the grass to listen to the palaver. On returning to their homes, the firing of muskets and the beating of drums never cease during the remainder of the day. The green and shaded banks of the brook that flows through their suburb, are, on Sundays especially, covered with clothes bleaching and drying; that day, above all others, being chosen by the Mandingo wives to execute their labours as washerwomen."

KROOMEN. The Kroo Republic, on the Grain Coast, lies at a distance of about 400 miles to the south of Sierra Leone, to the N. and W. of Cape Palmas. Five principal towns, each the metropolis of a district under different headmen, are united for common protection. One of the most remarkable peculiarities of this singular people is their detestation of slavery. They are very different from all the other inhabitants of West Africa in this respect; but it will probably be found on investigation, that this aversion to slavery has arisen not so much from a difference in character as from some exceptional circumstances in which they have been placed. To an universal rule obtaining through all the kingdoms of the West Coast, the Kroos alone form an exception; and as white men, like themselves, detest slavery, and are everywhere engaged in the suppression of slavery, the Kroos naturally seek the society of the white man. "Krooman," they say, "no can live from white man; white man love work, Krooman love work; white man no slave, Krooman no slave; where white man go, there Krooman must come."

Paddling his shallow and sharp canoe, scooped from a single tree, the Krooman performs the long voyage from his own country to the English settlement, and encounters many dangers before he reaches the place chosen by him for long and severe exertions, voluntarily sought and cheerfully endured. So light and frail is his canoe that it is frequently overturned at sea, and is constantly full of water; but he swims like a fish by its side, rights it, and gets into it again, nothing the worse for the wetting, since he wears no clothes and is not encumbered with worldly goods of any description. In seeking the society of the white man, the Kroo has an eye to wealth. He is bent on making money. On his arrival at Freetown, he binds himself as an apprentice, and learns some business. In a few years, he commences business on his own account. He sometimes contrives to earn as much as twenty shillings a month, of which he spends one, carefully hoarding up the other nineteen. His tastes are simple; his wants few. In the single item of clothing he saves a fortune, for he pays no tailor's bills. Intent on adding to his store, his industry never flags, and what he cannot obtain by honest labour he scruples not to get possession of by theft. At the age of forty, he generally finds himself the owner of as many pounds sterling, and he has then attained what, to him, is the summit of earthly grandeur. He lays out his coin in marketable articles, for his money would be useless to him in his native country, and having done this, he returns to live for the rest of his days in the midst of his countrymen, with much the same feelings as an Anglo-Indian returning home laden with wealth, the reward of unremitting toil in a foreign land.

There are no Kroo women in Sierra Leone. The Kroos are practical political economists, of the Malthusian school, and do not marry until mature age and adequate income justify them in incurring the responsibilities of matrimonial life. Kroo Town, therefore, presents a solitary instance of a bachelor village. In an evening you may see groups of men with the smallest possible quantity of clothing on their persons, squatting together or lying drowsily on the bare ground, courting sleep after their day's work; but no woman can be seen amongst them. Superior in intellect to the generality of the natives of the Western Coast, the Kroos are despised by the Settlers and Maroons. They preserve the distinctness of their community. They are perfectly exclusive. None but Kroo men may live in Kroo Town; and strangers are seldom permitted to visit it. Their peculiar habits are rigidly maintained. No innovation is permitted on any account. In regard to religion, they are Pagans; and it is stated, on good authority, that there has never yet been an instance of one of them being converted to Christianity.

EUROPEANS. The European residents at Sierra Leone are, generally speaking, our own countrymen, who are either engaged in commerce or hold appointments under the Colonial Government. Besides these, there are, of course, the missionaries and other clergymen of the Church of England with their wives and families, and also ministers of some of the dissenting bodies. The Krooman who compares his countrymen to the white men, is seldom aware how striking is the resemblance between the two. Both are voluntary colonists. Both are migratory. Both settle in the colony in the hope of earning money. Both leave it and return home when the desired money has been earned. To this rule the clergy and the dissenting ministers are the sole exceptions. Their object in going to Sierra Leone is a nobler and a higher one. There is no opportunity for them to amass wealth, if, even, they desired it. But they have bestowed on Sierra Leone benefits, which all the wealth of the Indies could not have purchased. They have laid deep the foundations of peace, prosperity, and security, by establishing amongst a once heathen population the religion of Jesus Christ; and that religion has proved to be in Sierra Leone as elsewhere, "the power of God unto salvation to every one that believeth."

It is of missionary work that I am about to write; of missionary work carried on in the midst of much difficulty, in the face of much opposition; of missionary work steadily continued during a long course of years, in spite of the ridicule of faithless Christians in England, who, notwithstanding the marvellous results that have been achieved, still persist in denying the truth of facts patent to the whole world. The missionary history of Sierra Leone proves, beyond all doubt, that the work done there by the zealous disciples of the Lord Jesus Christ, is a work that bears on it the impress of the Divine approval; a work destined to endure throughout everlasting ages.

LIBERATED SLAVES. The great mass of the population of Freetown, and the inhabitants of the rest of the Peninsula, who do not come under any of the foregoing five designations, are either liberated slaves or the descendants of liberated slaves. They have been rescued by the bravery of British sailors from the pestilential atmosphere of the slave ship, and have been landed as free men and women on British territory. It was for the distinct purpose of providing a refuge for these unhappy slaves, when England commenced her war upon the slave trade, that the colony was selected by the British Government for their abode, as free subjects of the

British crown. It is still maintained for that object; and must be maintained so long as the cupidity of man tempts him to obtain wealth by the abominable traffic which has rendered desolate so many beautiful regions in Africa.

It would not be easy to describe the liberated Africans of Sierra Leone. There are to be found amongst them the discordant elements of many savage tribes; the Akoo, the Ibbo, the Bassa, the Papaw; the Congo, the Calabar, the Coromantin, the Bonny, and many others. All these, when they are landed in the colony, are complete savages; but the traces of barbarism are deeper in some tribes than in others. The face of the Akoo is gashed deeply in perpendicular lines, leaving cicatrices of a lighter colour. The Ibbos also cut their persons, scoring the face, arms, back, and breast. The face of the Bassa is chopped, apparently at random; and the patterns embossed on the backs of the Bassa women are so wonderfully contrived that the skin projects from the wounds as though skeins of thread were inserted beneath to raise it. When landed from the slave ship, the captive is generally quite destitute of clothing, and has to be taught the necessity for decent covering. The men receive from the colonial authorities a plot of ground, a few implements of husbandry, and a small sum of money each week for a short time, until they are able to earn money for their support. Many of them, like savages, pass their lives in almost complete idleness; contenting themselves with a few days' labour to prepare the ground for the reception of cassada, plaintain, and earthnuts. Bountiful nature does the rest, and furnishes them with an abundant supply of everything which they require for their sustenance. Some, more active and more thoughtful, attend the market at Freetown, and selling the produce of their farms realize a good deal of money. Many of the women sell fish of various kinds; snappers and ten-pounders, gropers and old wives, cavallers and jumping fish, mullets and soles. When the liberated negro has acquired habits of industry, and has tasted the pleasures of civilized life, he and his family will regularly attend the market, even when he lives at a distance of ten or twelve miles from the town, and will be satisfied if he realizes by the sale of his goods even the most trifling profit. Some of the liberated negroes have risen far above their fellows, and have become useful and expert tradesmen. Tailors are to be seen, who, until they were rescued from the slave ship, never thought of wearing a coat, much less of making one. Carpenters, masons, and blacksmiths work in a manner which would not be discreditable to Europeans. There are many instances of liberated negroes or their immediate descendants amassing great wealth by their exertions, and rising to be respectable and influential members of society.

Some of them have become, as we shall see in the course of this narrative, highly educated men and exemplary clergymen. Those who engage in business, appear fonder of embarking in trading speculations than of plodding at any occupation that requires industry and perseverance. The author of "A Residence in Sierra Leone," in concluding an account of these liberated Africans, says:—"I must say, that, all circumstances considered, it is a matter of astonishment to me that there has been so much progress in civilization, though I am well aware the general opinion is quite opposed to mine. But indeed the difficulty, nay, the impossibility of rooting out the idolatry, superstitions, and barbarous practices of those grown up before they came here, or of teaching humanized habits to any except the mere infants amongst them, is perfectly beyond comprehension to those who have never tried to tame or teach an ignorant savage."

This brief description of Sierra Leone, its climate, and its inhabitants, will, it is to be hoped, prepare the reader to understand the following narrative of the missionary work which has for more than half a century been carried on there by the Church Missionary Society.

CHAPTER II.

THE WAR AGAINST SLAVERY.

> "Deem our nation brutes no longer,
>   Till some reason ye shall find
> Worthier of regard and stronger
>   Than the colour of our kind.
> Slaves of gold, whose sordid dealings
>   Tarnish all your boasted powers,
> Prove that you have human feelings,
>   Ere you proudly question ours."—COWPER.

WE shall now consider the circumstances under which Sierra Leone became a British Colony: the refuge and home of liberated Africans, and the country in which the chains of the great slave-dealer Satan, were broken asunder by the Almighty power of the Redeemer.

In the year 1765, Mr. William Sharp, an eminent surgeon, resided in London. He was the elder brother of Mr. Granville Sharp, who at that time held a subordinate situation in the Ordnance office. One morning as Mr. Granville Sharp was leaving his brother's surgery in Mincing lane, he met an African named Jonathan Strong. The poor black was evidently very ill, and in great need of medical advice and careful treatment. Mr. Sharp entered into conversation with him and learned that he was a slave. His master was a lawyer of Barbadoes, named David Lisle. This David Lisle had treated Strong most barbarously, had beaten him violently on the head—so violently as to cause the loss of one of his eyes—and after beating him had turned him out of doors. By the unremitting kindness of the two brothers Sharp, the negro was soon restored to health and placed in the service of a respectable apothecary, named Brown, in Fenchurch street. There his former master, Lisle, found him at the end of two years; and perceiving that he was in good health, and able to work, claimed him as his property. Resistance being made, two officers were called, and Strong was delivered into custody and sent to prison. From his prison cell, he wrote to his benefactor Mr. Granville Sharp, relating the circumstances of his arrest and imprisonment. Mr. Sharp at once lodged an information before the Lord Mayor of London, to the effect that the African had been imprisoned without a warrant, and sued that all persons concerned in the transaction might be summoned to account for their conduct. Thus in the providence of God, the sympathies of Mr. Sharp were excited in behalf of the oppressed negro, and the first blow was struck at the slave trade.

When the day appointed for the hearing of the case arrived, Mr. Sharp attended at the Mansion House; the African was produced, and two persons appeared to claim him. One of these was a notary public, who alleged that he had purchased him for £30 from David Lisle, and who produced the bill of sale; the other was the master of the ship on board of which the negro was to be taken to Jamaica: the agreement being that David Lisle was to receive £30 when the negro was placed on board. The Lord Mayor having heard the case argued, decided that Jonathan Strong had committed no offence against the laws of the land, that he had been illegally imprisoned, and that, therefore, he was to be immediately discharged from custody. The moment that the negro quitted the court, David Lisle seized him, and expressed his determination to obtain possession of his person. Mr. Sharp again interfered, and by threatening to proceed against Lisle for an assault, induced him to forego his resolution of capturing the negro, who, for a time, obtained shelter in Mr. Sharp's house. A few days after this occurrence, Mr. Sharp was served with a writ charging him with robbing David Lisle of a negro slave.

Law proceedings now commenced. Mr. Sharp employed as counsel, Sir James Eyre, an eminent lawyer, but his view of the case was most discouraging. He referred his client to an opinion given in 1729 by the Attorney and Solicitor-General of the time, in which they affirmed that "a slave by coming from the West Indies to Great Britain or

Ireland, either with or without his master, does *not* become free, and that his master might legally compel him to return to the plantations."

In the face of such a document Sir James Eyre said the case could not be defended; and in this opinion Lord Chief Justice Mansfield concurred.

Mr. Sharp, however, was not to be daunted. His professional adviser had given up his case as hopeless; but in spite of this discouraging fact, he resolved that he would attempt the defence of the case himself. He accordingly gave himself up to the study of those points of British law which have reference to the liberty of the subject, and pursued his study with intense application for two whole years. Step by step he was led on to a settled persuasion of the illegality of any attempt to carry out the practice of slavery in England; as well as to a settled conviction of the utter sinfulness of slave holding: and on the 18th of February, 1772, he addressed a letter to Lord North, calling upon him to put an end to such monstrous injustice, and reminding him of the criminal nature of slavery. Mr. Sharp had very little to encourage him in the performance of his self-imposed task. All the most eminent men of the legal profession were of opinion that as the law then stood, he had no ground for proceeding with his suit.

Lisle seeing Mr. Sharp's determined character, endeavoured, but in vain, to compromise the matter; and then on various pretexts sought to have the case adjourned, so that before the time for final adjudication had arrived, Mr. Sharp had completed a pamphlet which he circulated largely amongst lawyers. Such was the effect of this pamphlet on the barristers and other lawyers who were interested in the case, that Lisle thought it prudent to abandon the suit and withdraw his claim on the negro. What became of Jonathan Strong we are not told. Mr. Sharp's pamphlet was entitled, "The Injustice of tolerating Slavery in England." In it he affirmed, contrary to the prevailing opinion at the time, that a negro is neither of a base nature, nor is he a "thing," as he has been termed by slave holders, but one on whom nature had bestowed the privilege of humanity, and who was entitled whilst in England to an equal participation with other men in the protective power of the law.

About this time Mr. Sharp addressed his memorable letter to the Archbishop of Canterbury, in which, after entreating His Grace to devise some means of putting a stop to the dangerous increase of slaves in the kingdom, he says:—"I am myself convinced that nothing can thrive which is in any way concerned in that unjust trade. I have known several instances which were strong proofs to me of the judgments of God, even in this world, against such a destructive and iniquitous traffic."

Various cases of oppressed negroes continued

from time to time to occupy the attention of Mr. Sharp. In one of these cases, that of the slave Lewis, Lord Mansfield so delivered his judgment, that whilst he discharged the slave, he carefully avoided expressing any opinion on the great principle in question.

At last the particular case arose on which this long-contested point was to be finally decided—the case of the negro Somerset.

Somerset had been brought to England by a Mr. Stewart, and on his arrival in England, had run away from his master. His retreat, however, was discovered; he was seized, by Mr. Stewart's orders, and conveyed on board of a ship bound for Jamaica. He contrived, somehow, to make his case known to Mr. Sharp, who again stood forward as the friend of the oppressed negro. The matter came before the courts of law; arguments of counsel on both sides were heard; repeated adjournments took place, until, at last, on the 22nd of June, 1772, Lord Chief Justice Mansfield pronounced his memorable decision, which has never been reversed. "Tracing the subject," he said, "to natural principles, the claim of slavery never can be supported. The power claimed never was in use here, or acknowledged by the laws." From that time to this it has been a fixed principle in British law, that as soon as any slave sets foot on any part of the British dominions, he becomes *free*.

It was not intended by the Almighty Disposer of events that the results of this glorious victory over the principle of slavery should be circumscribed within the limits of the British Isles. The conflict with the slave trade, which had commenced in England, was to be continued in Africa.

Before, however, we enter on this portion of the narrative, let us briefly inquire into a few of the leading facts connected with the slave trade.

Sir Fowell Buxton, in his valuable work on the "Slave Trade and its Remedy," calculated, from accurate sources of information, that at the time he wrote, (1840,) the number of slaves annually imported into Brazil was 78,331; and into Cuba, 60,000. Besides these, he calculated the number rescued annually from slave ships, on their way to either of these settlements, at 8294; and of those who were lost from various casualties on the passage, such as shipwreck, suicide, or being thrown into the sea during a chase, a failure of provisions, or scarcity of water, he supposes there were not less than 3375; thus making a total of 150,000 human beings annually conveyed from Africa across the Atlantic, and sold as slaves. This, however, is believed to be a very low estimate. Captain Maclean, for several years Governor of Cape Coast Castle, on the Gold Coast, says:—"In the year 1834, I have every reason to believe that the number of slaves carried off from the Bights of Benin and Biafra amounted to 140,000." This statement had reference only to that part of the coast which was under his own immediate observation. In 1838, he found there were on the same coast 200 slave vessels under Portuguese colours. Mr. Mc Queen, who visited the slave colonies, and made his observations on the spot, rates the slave trade of Brazil at 90,000 annually, and that of Cuba and Porto Rico at 100,000, which, together with 6146 actually captured in 1837, make a total of 196,146.

There is another method of calculating, which raises the estimate still higher; that by the quantity and value of goods manufactured expressly and exclusively to be bartered for slaves. The value of Manchester cottons manufactured in 1836, exclusively for the slave trade, and suited only to that trade, was £250,000; whilst the amount of goods in the same year intended for the legitimate trade to Africa, was only £150,000. Now, as each slave averages £4 sterling for his cost price, £250,000 worth of cotton purchased 62,500 slaves; but as it it is stated, on good authority, that only one-third of the slaves are obtained by barter, we shall have 187,500 as the real number obtained. To these must be added the product of goods supplied from Glasgow, ammunition and fire-arms manufactured largely for the slave trade alone, American arms and goods, and East Indian goods which are also employed for the purpose of barter, all of which, if taken into calculation, will raise the total to 250,000.

Such is the nefarious trade once carried on by those who called themselves Christians. It is not at all surprising that the Mohammedans should lend their help to afflict the poor Africans. They have slave markets in Morocco, Tunis, Tripoli, Egypt, Turkey, Persia, and Arabia; and their trade is carried on both on the eastern coast of Africa, and across the Great Desert of Sahara. It is calculated that, thirty years ago, Africa was drained of 30,000 of her inhabitants annually by the coast trade, and of at least 20,000 by the caravan trade, making a total of 50,000, to be added to the 250,000 victims of the trade carried on by Christian nations. Compared with what it was half a century ago, the slave trade is now very insignificant; but even now, it is carried on to an extent which would be incredible, if our information were not derived from sources, the accuracy of which it is impossible to doubt.* The traffic in slaves was necessarily

* Thirty years ago, the slave trade was carried on very boldly, in spite of every effort made by the British Government. Madame Ida Pfeiffer says:—"On the same evening, (3rd January, 1847,) we saw a vessel, which our captain affirmed was a slaver, run into the bay. It kept as far as possible from the fort, and cast anchor at the most outward extremity of the bay. As the night was clear and moonlight, we walked late upon deck, when, sure enongh, we saw little boats laden with negroes, pulling in shore. An officer, indeed, came from the fort to inquire into the doings of this suspicious craft, but the owner seemed to afford him a satisfactory account, for he

attended with circumstances of the most fearful cruelty.

First of all the slaves were hunted down and seized. The native chiefs, for gain, made incursions into the country, and provided the dealers with the number of individuals which they required. At the marriage of the Sultan of Mandara's daughter and the Sheik of Bonroo's son, the dower was to be the result of a slave hunting expedition into the Kerdy country by the united forces of these chiefs. Three thousand wretches were made slaves, and probably double the number were sacrificed in obtaining them.

In 1823 King Boatswain, being in debt to a French slaver who required young slaves, selected a peaceable tribe near the Queahs, made an assault at night on them whilst they were asleep, murdered in one hour every adult male and female as well as the very young children, and reserved the boys and girls to pay the Frenchman. When the slaves had been seized and secured they were marched

---

left the ship, and the slaves continued during the whole night to be quietly and undisturbedly smuggled in as before.

"On the morning of the 4th of January, as we sailed past the vessel, we beheld a great number of the poor creatures still standing upon the deck. Our captain inquired of the slave-dealer how many slaves he had on board, and we learned with astonishment that the number amounted to 670. Much has already been said and written upon this horrible trade; it is everywhere execrated, and looked upon as a blot on the human race, and yet it still continues to flourish."—*A Woman's Journey round the World.*

down to the coast. Fastened by the leg and sometimes also by the neck, they were made to walk a distance of five hundred miles and more, the whip being freely used to urge them on. The disabled were left to perish, and, of course, large numbers died. Denham bivouacked on a spot where more than a hundred skeletons were lying, and after a journey of twenty-six miles, computed that a hundred and seven more skeletons were strewed along the track. Thirty-six per cent. was the average loss of every caravan of slaves.

On arriving at the coast, if no slaver were in sight, the slaves were shut up in crowded yards heavily ironed and half starved. It was not uncommon for the cargo to be then weeded of the old, diseased, and infirm (to avoid the cost of their maintenance) by throwing them into the river.

After this came the horrors of the voyage. All other sufferings yielded to this. Legislative enactments were certainly passed regulating the size of the ships and the proportion of stowage, but these enactments were constantly disregarded. The mortality averaged from one-third to one-half of the slaves. In a voyage of 4000 miles, liable to calms, contrary winds, and storms, with no port to run into, provisions often failed, and the mortality arising from hunger, thirst, heat, filth, disease, and brutal treatment all combined, was necessarily very great. It could hardly have been otherwise even if provisions had been abundant, when four hundred human beings were crammed into a space not high enough to sit up or turn themselves in, close, dark, fœtid, and foul with pestilential vapour, for more than six weeks at a time. "When we mounted the decks" (of a Spanish slaver) says Dr. Walsh in his Notices of Brazil, "we found her full of slaves. She had taken on board five hundred and sixty two, and had been out seventeen days, during which she lost fifty-five. The slaves were all enclosed under grated hatchways between decks. The space was so low that they sat between each other's legs, and were stowed so close together that there was no possibility of their lying down, or at all changing their position by night or day. As they belonged to different individuals, they were all branded like sheep with their owners' marks of different forms. These were impressed under their breasts or on their arms, and as the mate informed me with perfect indifference, '*burned with the red-hot iron.*'"

And yet advocates of slavery, when these facts were brought to light, had the assurance to declare, even in Parliament, that the passage across to America was one of the happiest periods in the negro's life.

It seems strange, indeed, that this iniquitous traffic in human beings should ever have been tolerated by men who had been taught the Gospel of the Divine Saviour. But so, unhappily, it was. The slave trade was thought to be quite lawful, was not considered to be unchristian. Respectable English merchants were not ashamed of engaging in it. To be a dealer in slaves did not disqualify a man for even the highest place in British society, and did not render him liable to be cut off from membership with the Christian Church.

In 1786—fourteen years after the decision in Somerset's case—the number of destitute negroes in London had become very considerable. Some had been turned adrift by their masters in consequence of Lord Mansfield's decision. Many had served in the Army and Navy during the American war; and having spent all their earnings had fallen into extreme poverty. Unable to earn their bread, and having no parish to fall back upon, they wandered about the streets in the utmost destitution. All who heard of Mr. Sharp, and there were few who had not heard of him, flocked to him; and obtained from him temporary relief out of a fund which he had collected for the purpose. This fund, however, in time began to be exhausted, and it was considered advisable to adopt some plan by which the wants of these destitute negroes might be permanently relieved.

Under these circumstances, it was proposed by a Mr. Smeatham, who had lived for some time in Sierra Leone, that a free settlement for negroes should be formed in that part of Western Africa. Mr. Smeatham died before his plan could be matured; but it was adopted by Mr. Sharp, who brought the matter before the notice of the Government; and preparations were made without delay to transport these poor Africans to their own country. The transports sailed from England under convoy of the "Nautilus" sloop of war, on the 8th of April, 1787.

Four hundred negroes were sent out, and to these were added sixty Europeans, most of whom were women. Great unhealthiness prevailed on board during the passage, owing principally to disorders brought on board, and aggravated by subsequent intemperance. In consequence, too, of many unfortunate delays, the transports arrived at Sierra Leone during the rainy season; so that many who landed from them died soon after landing. In the course of twelve months, their number was reduced to one half of what it was when they left England. Some who survived fled into the interior and were never heard of again. Many, however, remained in the colony, and began to build a town. Out of two hundred settlers, only five or six died during the second year; and the survivors managed to support themselves comfortably without any very great exertion. Occasionally, a spirit of restlessness and dissatisfaction manifested itself, and some left the colony to seek their fortunes in the interior.

During these periods of discontent, the number of those who left was so great, that there was every danger of the colony being broken up. At this critical time, an English vessel arrived with a plentiful supply of provisions and other necessaries for the use of the colonists. This had the effect of inducing some who had left the colony to return; whilst it made those who had remained more satisfied with their condition. At the same time a confirmation of the original grant of land composing the colony was obtained from Naimbanna, the king of Sierra Leone, who lived on the small island of Rohanna.

Towards the end of 1789, when prosperity seemed to have set in, the colonists received a formal notice from the great council of a neighbouring chief, that he had resolved on burning their town in retaliation for some injury inflicted on his capital by the crew of an English ship of war. Three days were allowed them for the removal of their goods, and at the expiration of the three days the town was mercilessly set on fire. Utter ruin now threatened the colonists, but Providence again interfered on their behalf.

A company had been formed in England, called the St. George's Bay Company, St. George being the name of one of the bays on the northern coast of Sierra Leone; and an agent from the company, Mr. Falconbridge, was despatched in 1790 with a commission to examine and report upon the state of the colony. He was also commissioned to afford temporary relief to the sufferers from the late disaster, until the grant of a Charter, for which application had been made to King George III., should enable the directors to take measures to insure the protection of the colonists. Mr. Falconbridge, on his arrival, commenced the formation of a settlement at Fourah Bay. In honour of Mr. Granville Sharp, the negro's friend, the settlement was called Granville Town; and as favourable accounts of Sierra Leone began to be circulated in England, as soon as the St. George's Bay Company had obtained their Charter, a considerable amount of money was raised as capital, with which to carry on the trade of the settlement.

The directors now began to consider what would be the best means of adding to the number of the colonists; and whilst this matter was under consideration, a negro named Peters arrived in England from Nova Scotia, as a delegate from a number of his countrymen, who had been induced to settle in that country after the American War. These men had been encouraged to enlist in the British army by the King's proclamation of freedom to all slaves who would join the Royal standard; and after the war they were carried to Nova Scotia, where they were promised allotments of land, which, it appears, they never received. They were now anxious to join the new colony at Sierra Leone; and the Government, on being applied to, engaged to defray the expenses of their passage from Nova Scotia. Lieutenant Clarkson, of the Royal Navy, was appointed to convey the new colonists to Sierra Leone; and on their arrival each was to receive an allotment of twenty acres of land, on entering into a stipulation to conform to all the laws and regulations of the colony.

Lieutenant Clarkson set sail from England on August 19th, 1791; and on arriving at Nova Scotia he found that the number of emigrants to be conveyed to Africa was 1196, instead of between three and four hundred, as their delegate had stated. Sixteen vessels were procured for their accommodation; and on their arrival at Sierra Leone, in March 1792, there were 1131 negroes landed in the colony, sixty-five having died on the passage. Just before the arrival of the Nova Scotia negroes, a vessel had arrived from England, bringing to the colony more than a hundred Europeans. Many of these were artisans and farmers; some were soldiers, with their wives and children.

Thus was the colony gradually peopled, and a foundation was laid for the labours of the Church Missionary Society.

The first thing done by the new comers, was to set to work and build a new town, which, according to the instructions of the directors, was to be called Freetown.

During the rainy season, which began in May, the colonists were severely tried by fever, which attacked all indiscriminately, both Europeans and Africans. Nearly half the Europeans and a tenth of the Nova Scotians died during this unhealthy season. The year 1793 was more favourable than the preceding one had been. Schools were opened for the education of the children; and the colonists having become more accustomed to the climate, began to settle down comfortably in their new homes.

Serious discontent, however, broke out among them. Complaints were made against the Governor. He was charged with acts of oppression and injustice; and two of the colonists were sent to England as delegates, to lay their case before the directors. The decision of the directors was entirely in favour of the Governor; which so exasperated the colonists that a formidable insurrection broke out. The very existence of the colony was at stake. Happily, however, the outbreak was suppressed without bloodshed. Six of the ringleaders were banished, and peace was restored.

A more formidable disaster followed. War between England and France having been declared in 1793, a French squadron appeared in the river Sierra Leone, on the 28th of September 1794; and Freetown was plundered and destroyed with circumstances of the greatest barbarity, and without any resistance on the part of the colonists. This visitation, severe as it was, ultimately proved of the greatest benefit to the colony. The voice of dissension was hushed; and the spirited exertions of the Company in retrieving the disasters which had been occasioned by the French, were productive of improvements which, in more peaceful times, would, perhaps, never have been thought of.

In 1798 Freetown contained about 300 dwelling houses, besides several public buildings. Three quays were constructed; and the Government House was built on an eminence commanding the harbour, and protected by six pieces of cannon. The inhabitants of the colony now amounted to 1200, half of whom were farmers; the rest were mechanics, retail shopkeepers, fishermen, and seamen. Every day, the natives who lived in the neighbourhood, were to be seen in numbers, varying from one to two hundred, trading with the colonists, and exchanging the products of Africa for the manufactures of Great Britain.

With prosperity discontent returned. The Nova Scotians broke out again into insurrection, and threatened to destroy not only the power but the lives of the officers who were entrusted with the government of the colony. Under these trying circumstances, the directors applied for and obtained a new Charter, by which the power placed in the hands of the Governor and Council was greatly increased, the settlement became an independent colony, and the Governor was charged with the criminal as well as the civil jurisdiction. Before this Charter arrived, however, the insurgents considering that no time was to be lost, were about to carry their sanguinary plans into execution, when the Providence of God interposed to deliver the loyal portion of the community from certain destruction, and preserved this portion of Africa to become in future times the theatre of great spiritual exploits.

The "Asia" transport unexpectedly appeared in the river, having on board 550 Maroons, including women and children, from Nova Scotia, together with a detachment of the 24th Regiment. The services of the soldiers were soon put into requisition. The insurgents were attacked and routed. Two of them were killed, and thirty-five were taken prisoners. Of the thirty-five, three were tried and executed for rebellion, and the rest were expelled the colony.

Peace again smiled on Sierra Leone. The Maroons settled at Granville Town. Farms were allotted to them, and they soon built a neat town, and began to cultivate their land. The Company received from Parliament an indemnity for their losses, and £5000 to build a fort.

In November, 1801, peace was again disturbed. A body of natives headed by two of the still restless Nova Scotians, suddenly attacked the Governor's house. They were, however, repulsed, and a reinforcement of soldiers having arrived from Goree, order was for a time restored.

Once more an attempt was made to promote rebellion. In March, 1802, four hundred natives, headed by eleven of the banished Nova Scotians, invaded the colony. Another struggle took place, and again the rebels were repulsed with great loss. But so trying had these repeated attacks become to the loyal portion of the colonists, that they seriously thought of abandoning their farms and leaving the settlement for ever.

A very important change now took place in the government of the colony. The contest between the Nova Scotian rebels and the colonial authorities attracted the attention of Parliament. An inquiry into the history and circumstances of the colony was ordered, and the result of this inquiry was a Report, in which the Parliamentary Committee recommended the suppression of the Sierra Leone Company, and the transfer of the civil and military authority in the settlement to the British Crown. A Bill to that effect passed both Houses, and on the 8th of August, 1807, received the Royal assent. On the 1st of January, 1808, the Company surrendered its authority to the Crown, and the colony entered on a new chapter in its history.

In April, 1807, a new Company had been formed, having for its object the improvement of Africa, and the civilization of its inhabitants. It was called "The African Institution." Of this Company, his Royal Highness the Duke of Gloucester was patron and president. On the dissolution of the Sierra Leone Company, the British Government placed the colony under the management of the African Institution; and by this new Society its affairs were managed until 1827, when the Institution brought its useful labours to a close, and Sierra Leone was again placed under the control of the Crown.

The Committee of the African Institution laboured most energetically to promote the welfare of the inhabitants of Sierra Leone. Schools were established throughout the colony; the study of the native languages was encouraged; the growth of cotton, indigo, rice, and coffee, was promoted, and even the manufacture of silk was attempted. Everything was done to diffuse a taste for agriculture, and to lead the people to engage in lawful commerce; but so long as the slave trade, which had been abandoned by Great Britain in 1807, was carried on by the other maritime nations of Europe, the members of the African Institution found that their labours for the social regeneration of Africa were productive of comparatively little good. In spite of every protest, the slave trade continued to be carried on by the ships of France, Spain, and Portugal. Every effort was made by the directors of the Institution to mitigate the horrors of the slave trade, and the reports annually published by them materially influenced public opinion.

On the 10th of May, 1822, at a meeting held in Freemason's Hall, under the presidency of the Duke of Gloucester, Lord Calthorpe in moving a vote of thanks to the Board of Directors for their "unceasing attention to the objects of the Institution," during the previous year, said:—"When we consider the circumstances which had brought the situation of Africa more particularly under the observation of this country, and within the pale of our strongest sympathies, and above all, the atrocities which have been committed for centuries against the population of that vast continent by subjects of Great Britain, then indeed it became still more our bounden duty to labour to ameliorate the condition of the African race, not only as an object worthy of the solicitude of philanthropy, and calling for the voluntary display of Christian kindness, but because our past conduct imposed on us a solemn and indispensable obligation to mitigate evils which we had been the principal instruments in inflicting. * * * * The necessity of the most active endeavours on behalf of Africa must be universally admitted. We have made them, but we have to lament their comparative inefficiency, owing to their not having been as fully seconded as they ought to have been by Foreign Powers."

At the same meeting Mr. Wilberforce said:— "Only a few years ago they had consoled themselves with the hope that the abolition of the slave trade was carried, that the powers of Europe would co-operate, as they had promised, in completely extinguishing this traffic on the part of their subjects. Unhappily, however, this sanguine and, as they had thought, well-founded expectation had been disappointed. They were bound, nevertheless, to proceed onwards in their course. They were called upon by every sacred principle to go on without desponding, acting as they were on principles, and impelled by motives which carried with them their own reward; and which would in their proper time be rewarded, even if their efforts had been less successful, or had they not been successful at all."

Mr. Brougham—afterwards Lord Brougham— —then addressed the meeting, and in an eloquent speech moved the adoption of the following resolution:—"That this meeting views with peculiar satisfaction, not only the desire manifested by the Government and legislature of the United States of America to co-operate with Great Britain in putting an end to the slave trade, but above all the bright example which they have recently held forth to all other states in being the foremost to declare that trade to be piracy." *

These extracts may serve to show the depth of the feeling which influenced the Directors of the African Institution against the slave trade and the opposition which they had to encounter. The resolution moved by Mr. Brougham, may also serve to point out the growth of that anti-slavery feeling in America, which in our own days culminated in a disastrous civil war, but which has ended in the triumphant victory of the anti-slavery principle, and in the liberation of the captives from their horrible and inhuman captivity.

The success of the Directors of the African Institution was by no means proportioned to their zeal and energy. For twenty years they toiled and struggled, until at last the conviction forced itself upon them, that in seeking merely the abolition of the slave trade, they were seeking only a partial accomplishment of the task which had been entrusted to them. The enemy of the slave trade, they considered, should aim at nothing less than the total extinction of slavery; and, acting on this conviction, they abandoned the field of conflict, leaving it to the Anti-Slavery Society, which had been called into existence in the year 1823, to destroy for ever the demon of slavery throughout the British dominions.

* Report of the Sixteenth Anniversary Meeting of the African Institution.

On the 28th of August, 1833, the Act for abolishing slavery throughout the whole British Empire received the royal assent; and from that day to this, the banner of Britain has waved only over free populations in every part of the world.

Let us now see how the circumstances above recorded, affected Sierra Leone and its inhabitants.

On the 23rd of May, 1806, an Act of Parliament was passed, called—"An Act to prevent the importation of slaves by any of His Majesty's subjects into any islands, colonies, plantations, or territories belonging to any foreign sovereign, state, or power."

This was followed by "An Act for the Abolition of the Slave Trade." The second and fourteenth sections of the Abolition Act provide that every vessel which, after the passing of the Act, shall have been fitted out for the purposes of the slave trade, together with all her boats, guns, tackle, apparel, and furniture, shall become forfeited, and may be seized by any officer of His Majesty's Customs or Excise, or by the commanders or officers of any of His Majesty's ships or vessels of war. It was further enacted, that the slaves found on board such vessels, should be entitled to their freedom, and the captor of them to certain bounties, which are specified.

These two Acts of Parliament gave rise to two Orders in Council, dated March 16th, 1808.

The first order appoints that "the collector or chief officer of the Customs, for the time being, in any of His Majesty's colonies, being Courts of Vice-Admiralty, shall receive, protect, and provide for all such negroes, natives of Africa, as shall have been or shall be condemned, either as prize of war, or forfeiture to the Crown, under the provision of the above Acts;" and directs the collector or chief officer to "receive all such negroes, and to provide suitably for their support and maintenance, subject to the directions of His Majesty, until such negroes can be entered, enlisted, apprenticed, or disposed of, according to the true meaning of the Acts."

The second order notifies that "as it is expedient that all slaves, or natives of Africa, taken as prize in or near the coast of Africa, or at any other place from which they can conveniently be carried thither, should then be prosecuted or adjudged, a Prize Court has been constituted at Sierra Leone, in Africa, for the trial and adjudication of any capture of slaves taken as prize, and of all ships in which the same shall be found, and of the cargoes therein laden."

It will at once be perceived what a mighty influence this order had on the destinies of Sierra Leone. It became, thenceforward, the great depôt for liberated slaves, who, on their landing in the colony, became the free subjects of the British Crown. Many of them, too, in due time, became earnest and faithful Christians in connexion with the British Church.

The population of the colony soon increased. In 1811, it amounted to nearly 4500, of whom more than half were liberated slaves. In 1817, there were 5130 negroes in the colony. Of these 284 had been born there; the rest had been liberated from slavery. In 1833, the entire population amounted to nearly 30,000. In the course of fourteen years, from 1819 to 1833, no fewer than 27,167 slaves had been liberated, and landed in the colony.

CHAPTER III.

THE PIONEERS.

"Faith is our battle-token;
Our leader all controls]:
Our trophies, fetters broken;
Our captives, ransom'd souls."—BICKERSTETH.

THE Church Missionary Society was founded amidst many difficulties and much opposition, in 1799. At that time, with the exception of what had been done by the few Danish missionaries who had been sent out to India by the Society for Promoting Christian Knowledge, nothing had been done by the Church of England to spread Christianity amongst the heathen. No English clergyman had ever gone forth to raise the standard of the Cross in Africa; and the vast heathen populations which dwelt within the limits of the British possessions in the East were utterly neglected by the church. In 1799 a few earnest men established the "Society for Missions to Africa and the East." In 1812 the name of the Society was changed to that which it has borne ever since,—"The Church Missionary Society for Africa and the East." This name was given to distinguish it from the Missionary Societies of the Protestant Dissenters, and to intimate that its proceedings would be conducted in strict conformity with the doctrines and discipline of the Church of England.

Africa having been selected by the Committee of the Society as the field in which missionary work should be commenced, it became necessary to consider carefully on what part of that vast continent the seed of the gospel should be first sown. There were many reasons which induced the Committee to send their first missionaries to Western Africa. Some of these reasons are alluded to in the instructions delivered by the Committee to them before their departure from England.

"The temporal misery of the whole world," the Committee said, "has been dreadfully aggravated by its intercourse with men who bear the name of Christians; but the Western coast of Africa, between the tropics, and more especially that part of it between the line and the tropic of Cancer, has not only, in common with other heathen countries, received from us our diseases and our vices, but it has ever been the chief theatre of the inhuman slave trade; and tens of thousands of its children have been annually torn from their dearest connexions to minister to the luxuries of men bearing the Christian name, and who had no more a right to exercise this violence than Africans had to depopulate our coast with a similar view. The wickedness and wretchedness consequent on this trade of blood have deeply and extensively infected these shores; and though Western Africa may justly charge her sufferings from this trade upon all Europe, directly or remotely, yet the British nation is now and has long been most deeply criminal. We desire, therefore, while we pray and labour for the removal of this evil, to make Western Africa the best remuneration in our power for its manifold wrongs."

Amongst the numerous tribes to be found in Western Africa, the Soosoos appeared to be the most likely to receive the instructions of missionaries with attention. They inhabited a tract of country extending from the river Kissee to the Rio Nunez. The Committee were directed in their selection of this tribe by the fact that Mr. Brunton, a Scotch missionary, had, after a residence of some years in the country, acquired the Soosoo language, and had offered to give the Church Missionary Society the benefit of his knowledge and experience. He was accordingly employed to prepare a grammar and vocabulary, and to compile such other books as might clearly set forth the doctrines of Christ. Mr. Brunton carried on his work with great diligence and in the course of time completed not only a grammar and vocabulary in the Soosoo language, but also a spelling book, the catechism, three dialogues on the subject of Christianity, and an abridgment of Scripture history and doctrine.

At the African Academy, at Clapham, were several Soosoo boys who had been brought from their own country to be educated, and when portions of Mr. Brunton's books were read to these boys, it was found that they perfectly understood them; and thus the fidelity and accuracy of these valuable works were completely tested. This was the first attempt ever made to reduce the languages of Western Africa to writing.

The Soosoo language was spoken throughout an immense tract of country in Western Africa. The Committee of the African Institution, in one of their reports, said, that "the Soosoo language is spoken very generally on the coast to about a hundred and fifty miles to the northward of Sierra Leone. It is also understood by a great part of the Foulah and Mandingo natives, and it is the vernacular tongue of the country of Jallonkadoo, a large kingdom, in the mountains of which the Niger is said to take its rise. It would not, therefore, be too large a calculation to suppose that it is spoken over a space of eight hundred or a thousand miles square, a space considerably larger than Great Britain."

The Committee had thus selected a field for operations amongst the heathen, and had obtained the means of declaring to them, in their own language, the wonderful works of God. The next step was to find men able and willing to undertake the arduous task of commencing the missionary work amongst the Soosoos. Applications were made to a large number of clergymen throughout England, and these clergymen were requested to recommend fit and proper persons to become labourers in the mission field. Men, however, were not to be found. The climate of West Africa was known to be generally fatal to Europeans; missionary work was known to be difficult and trying, even under the most favourable circumstances; and an opinion prevailed very extensively, that the negroes of Western Africa were by nature so nearly allied to brute beasts, that all attempts to elevate them in the social scale must prove fruitless, and all attempts to convert them to Christianity must end in grievous disappointment. At the time of which I am writing, our country was waging war in another part of Africa against the great military despot who had usurped the supreme authority in France. Sir Ralph Abercrombie had landed an army in Egypt to oppose the plans of Eastern conquest that had been formed by Napoleon Buonaparte. For this expedition there was no difficulty in procuring volunteers. Thousands were willing to die on the banks of the Nile in defence of their king and country. Not one came forward to risk his life in Western Africa in defence of the Christian faith. Not a single clergyman of the Church of England volunteered to go forth and preach the gospel to the Soosoos of Africa.

Failing to procure clergymen in England, the Committee turned to Germany, the country of Luther and Melancthon, the country that has produced many eminent ministers of Christ, many devoted, self-denying, zealous soldiers of the cross. There existed at Berlin an institution for the education of young men who intended to devote themselves to missionary work. Its president was the Rev. John Jœnicke. At the time that the existence of this institution became known to the Committee of the Church Missionary Society, there were only six students within its walls; bnt there were many who were anxious to be admitted to it, and who were only excluded because the slender finances of the institution could support no more than six. To this institution application was made, and after some correspondence with the Rev. John Jœnicke, two young men were selected as the Society's first missionaries, Melchior Renner, a native of the Duchy of Wurtemberg, and Peter Hartwig, a Prussian.

On their arrival in England they were sent to Mr. Greave's school, at Clapham, where they studied the Soosoo language, and held familiar intercourse with the Soosoo boys, of whom mention has been made above. Towards the close of the year 1803, Mr. Renner and Mr. Hartwig went to Germany and received Lutheran ordination. On their return to England they were finally accepted by the Committee as missionaries of the Society.*

On the 8th of March, 1804, the two missionaries sailed from Portsmouth, and after narrowly escaping from being captured by a French privateer, they arrived at Freetown, the capital of Sierra Leone, on the 14th of April.

At first they took up their abode at Freetown, with the intention of cultivating a more familiar acquaintance with the language, habits, and manners of the Soosoos, many of whom lived in and around Freetown. Both were, at times, grievously tried by attacks of fever; but from each attack they rallied, and as strength returned they resumed their labours. To enter into a particular account of these labours would weary the reader. The story is an oft-repeated one. The work of the missionary is everywhere the same. Man is everywhere by nature, sinful; inclined to do that which is evil. The message with which the missionary is entrusted is the same for all. Christ is everywhere found to be a Saviour and a Deliverer both from the guilt and power of sin. The two missionaries, therefore, whenever and wherever they could obtain access to the Soosoos, spoke of the love of God as shown in the atonement made by Christ, of the necessity of faith in Christ, and of the influence of

---

* The Society for Promoting Christian Knowledge had already employed Lutheran clergymen in India.

the Holy Spirit. Like the village pastor with whom Goldsmith has made us familiar, they—

"Allured to brighter worlds and led the way."

Brunton's books were distributed here and there. Occasionally, children, the offspring of the Nova Scotian and other settlers were baptized; but during the first year there could not be said to be any visible result of their work amongst the natives of the country.

In 1806 three new missionaries arrived from Europe. Like Renner and Hartwig, they had been sent from the Berlin Institution to London, and thence had been despatched to Africa. They were Gustavus Nyländer, a Pole; Leopold Butscher, a Suabian; and John Prasse, a native of Lusatia.

On the 12th of February, 1806, these three missionaries sailed from Liverpool. After encountering some severe weather, the vessel in which they sailed was stranded on a sand bank on the coast of Ireland, near Wexford, about four in the morning. It pleased God, however, to rescue them from the perils of the deep. They returned to England; and on the 22nd of April they embarked in another ship at Bristol. On the 25th the ship arrived at Falmouth, and waited there for some time to be taken under convoy. Whilst the missionaries were on shore at Falmouth the convoy came in sight, and the captain, without waiting for them or sending them any notice of his intention, put to sea. At the risk of their lives they followed the ship in an open boat, but the wind rose to a gale, and after tossing about for several hours, they were forced to return to Falmouth. Scarcely had they landed, when the wind suddenly changed, and the whole fleet was obliged to put back and come to an anchor. They accordingly got on board of their ship, sailed again, and reached Madeira safely on the 2nd of June. Here the captain died in a fit of apoplexy brought on by intemperance; and the British Consul thinking it his duty to detain the vessel until instructions could be obtained from her owners in England, the missionaries were obliged to remain at Madeira for four months, during which time they employed themselves in studying the Soosoo language. On the 17th of September they sailed from Madeira, and ten days after they landed in Sierra Leone.

It was the design of the Committee that the missionaries should form settlements amongst the natives, from which they should, as opportunity offered, make excursions amongst the neighbouring tribes; and from which they should ultimately, as their numbers increased, establish out-stations. Four of the five missionaries who were now in the country were directed to settle without delay in a Soosoo town on the Rio Pongas, where a friendly chief lived; whilst Mr. Nyländer was instructed to remain at Freetown, and there to discharge the duties of chaplain to the colonists.

At this point in our story we are reminded of the frailty of man, and of the utter uselessness of the missionary whose heart is not under the influence of Divine Grace. A dispute had arisen between Renner and Hartwig about seniority. No sooner had this been settled by the definite instructions of the Committee, than it was discovered that Hartwig had yielded to the temptation of encouraging and participating in the profits of the slave trade. It was also discovered that he had been guilty of several gross irregularities. Of course, as soon as this was proved to the satisfaction of the Committee, he was removed from his position. The tie which had bound him to his four missionary brethren was severed. He did not, however, leave the country; but continued to reside in the colony till 1815, just as missionary work in Western Africa had made a fresh start, and had entered on the glorious career which we see it running at the present time.

As the first duty of a historian is to be faithful, I do not shrink from this allusion to the misconduct of one who had been called to the high and holy office of the Christian missionary. But whilst a regard for truth compels me to record *this* incident, it compels me also to record, in this place, that such incidents have been rare in the annals of the

Church Missionary Society; that very few indeed of that large number of missionaries employed by the Society during the last sixty years of its existence have proved unworthy of confidence, or have failed to manifest in their lives the fruits of a living faith.

The missionaries being naturally anxious to commence their work amongst the Soosoos, Mr. Butscher, on the 15th of October, 1807, set out from Sierra Leone in a Company's ship for the Rio Pongas. In the neighbourhood of the Rio Pongas lived a chief named Fantimani, the father of one of the Soosoo boys who were receiving a Christian education at Clapham. Mr. Butscher went, as might have been expected, to visit this chief, and was most cordially received. Fantimani was not without some knowledge of the Christian religion. The historical portions of the New Testament were familiar to him; but he had not, on the occasion of Mr. Butscher's visit, yet abandoned the superstitious practices in which he had been brought up. One day Mr. Butscher found him in the act of making an offering, as he called it. He had laid two goats' horns on a tin dish, and kneeling before the dish, he was praying for the recovery of a sick person belonging to his tribe. He evidently considered the goats' horns to be a necessary accompaniment to the prayer.

A few days after Mr. Butscher's arrival, he went

with Fantimani to a place called Bassia, and visited the factory of Mr. Curtis, who expressed great delight at seeing a Christian missionary, and offered Mr. Butscher a large house to be used as a school, on condition that his own children should be educated in it. The house was a valuable one. It was two storeys high, about sixty feet by twenty in area, and well built of brick. Attached to it was a store nearly as large as the house itself. There were also four smaller houses adjoining it, and extensive gardens around it well stocked with lemon, plaintain, pine, and other trees. The water on the premises was good, and the river itself was fresh for eight months in the year. In the immediate neighbourhood was a small Soosoo town; and the country around was adorned by hundreds of palm trees, whose luxuriant foliage afforded a most desirable relief to the eye. The proposal of Mr. Curtis seemed quite providential. "The whole plan" wrote Mr. Renner to the Committee, "we must acknowledge is a kind present from God to the Mission; and we trust He will vouchsafe His blessing upon it, and make it both a hiding-place for us, and also a city which cannot be hid, from which may go forth light and truth to those who sit around in darkness and the shadow of death."

Mr. Butscher having had this handsome offer made to him, sent at once to communicate the intelligence to his brethren whom he had left behind him at Sierra Leone. A deed of gift was prepared and signed by Mr. Curtis, making over to Mr. Butscher "for his own benefit and use, the place called Bassia on the Rio Pongas;" and the other two missionaries Mr. Renner and Mr. Prasse having arrived at the new settlement, the mission to the Soosoos may be said to have been fairly established. As soon as the premises and grounds had been put into tolerable order, the following plan was drawn up and adopted:—

1. To have Divine Service every Sunday.

2. To abstain from traffic with the natives on Sunday.

3. To have family prayers every morning and evening; and to require the attendance of every one living on the premises who understood English.

4. To hold a prayer meeting in German on the first Monday of every month; German being the native language of the missionaries, and therefore more familiar to them than English.

5. To receive for instruction the children of all traders, on condition that the parents would provide food and clothing.

Everything now seemed to promise well. The missionaries had settled down in the very midst of the heathen; and by means of their schools and their books, they were preparing to diffuse around them some knowledge of the Gospel. Whilst, however, this work was in progress, one of the missionaries was suddenly called away from his work. Mr. Prasse, after a very short illness, died on the 23rd of January, 1809. He was a man of simple manners and of unassuming piety; and if his life had been spared he would doubtless have been a very useful missionary. But the Lord of the Harvest saw fit to summon him away in the midst of his labours, and he died amongst the heathen whom he ardently desired to convert to Christianity—the first martyr of the West African Church.

The Rev. Josiah Pratt, on receiving intelligence of Mr. Prasse's death, wrote to the surviving missionaries in these words:—" It grieves us much to hear of the death of Brother Prasse. This calls for patience and silent submission. It seems to our feeble minds extraordinary, that he should be led through a long course of preparation for the missionary work, and then be taken away, just as he was getting into the field of labour. But there are wise and gracious reasons for it, which we do not see. 'What I do thou knowest not now, but thou shalt know hereafter.' In the meantime—'Follow thou me;' this is our Lord's language to you and to us all. May this Providence, which has withdrawn one of your fellow-labourers, quicken your own diligence and zeal. May the same mind be more abundantly in you which was also in Christ Jesus when He said, 'I must work the works of him that sent me while it is day; the night cometh when no man can work.'"

The missionary staff was reinforced, in the month of August, 1809, by the arrival of the Rev. John Barneth, of Bernstorf, in Silesia, and the Rev. Charles Wenzel, of Breslau, also in Silesia; but early in the year 1810, Mr. Barneth, after recovering from repeated attacks of fever, at last sank from utter exhaustion, and was buried in the garden of the settlement at Bassia. He is represented as a man singularly amiable, and full of zeal for the service of God. Mr. Renner testifies concerning him, that "he was a lover of Jesus Christ, and an example to believers; for with full purpose of heart he clave unto the Lord."

Notwithstanding these severe trials, the remaining missionaries continued to labour faithfully. At Bassia, so many children were gradually gathered into the school, that an additional house, capable of accommodating fifty boys, was obtained, whilst the first house was reserved for girls.

The British and Foreign Bible Society was now called upon to co-operate with the Church Missionary Society, in carrying on this good work; and with its usual liberality, that Society made a grant of a hundred and fifty Bibles, and the same number of New Testaments, for the use of the settlers at Sierra Leone, together with fifty Bibles, and a hundred New Testaments, for the settlements on the Rio Pongas.

During the year 1811 the school at Bassia was enlarged to more than twice its former dimensions. It contained a hundred and twenty African children. Great confidence was reposed by the chiefs in the missionaries, and all the natives anxiously desired to see their children instructed in "the white man's book."

Two new missionaries, the Rev. John Wilhelm, and the Rev. Jonathan Klein, arrived at Sierra Leone from England in the month of December, 1811. On the 20th of January, 1812, they arrived at Bassia, where they were heartily welcomed. The missionaries were now six in number. Two of them had been sorely tried during the year 1811. Mrs. Nyländer and Mrs. Wenzel had both died; the former from the effects of excessive fatigue, the latter in her confinement.

The 25th of January, 1812, was a memorable day. The missionaries held a special meeting to implore the favour and assistance of Almighty God; and as Mr. Butscher had been ordered by the Committee to visit England, for the purpose of laying before them a particular account of the progress of the mission, his brethren took formal leave of him, and then made arrangements for the continuance of the work during his temporary absence. It was thought advisable that Mr. Wilhelm, with Mr. Renner, should remain at Bassia, whilst Mr. and Mrs. Klein, with Mr. Wenzel, should go to Canoffee.

Mr. Butscher arrived safely in England in May, 1812. He was accompanied by Richard Wilkinson, an African boy, one of his pupils at Bassia; and both were presented to the members of the Church Missionary Society, at the annual meeting held in London on the 19th of May. During Mr. Butschers' stay in London, the Committee held many conferences with him, and what they heard from his lips warranted them in expecting that, through the instrumentality of the mission now established, many great blessings would be conferred on Western Africa.

Hitherto, the labours of the missionaries had been limited to the education of the young. It was considered, however, that the time had now arrived when Africans of every age might be invited to hear the gospel preached to them. The Committee, therefore, earnestly enjoined Mr. Butscher and his brethren to preach as often as possible to adult Africans, and to imitate the missionaries of the early church in the simplicity and fervour of their discourses. Three laymen, John Quast, a boat-builder; Conrad Meissner, a smith; and Herman Meyer, a rope-maker, with their wives, were appointed to accompany Mr. Butscher, who, following the example of his lay brethren, also took to himself a wife.

As regular and speedy intercourse between the mission stations was desirable, the missionaries were authorized to procure a small vessel, of six or seven tons burden; and, in order to defray the expense of maintaining this vessel, the lay brethren were required, either to carry on lawful trade with the natives, or else to exchange their skilled labour for such commodities as the mission settlement might require. They were, however, specially cautioned against any attempt to accumulate private property. They were reminded that anything purchased by the Church Missionary Society, for the use of the mission, was the property of the Society. "So long," said the Committee, in their instructions, "as you are dependent on that body which has expended the public money in fitting you out, and supporting you, you cannot from its funds accumulate any property as your own; you owe yourselves and your all to the advancement of that cause, for the furtherance of which Christian charity has enabled the Society to send you among the heathen. If, by any prudence and economy, you can maintain each settlement for a less sum than that which the Society allows, any saving must not be regarded as your own, but you are bound to apply such savings to the diminution of the Society's expenses."

The Committee of the Church Missionary Society also, at this time, adopted the plan of redeeming a certain number of African children from slavery, and attaching them to the missionary settlements. They directed that for every settlement containing fifty children, eight should be redeemed at a sum not exceeding £10 for each child. The children were to be trained to act as servants; and they were to receive from the missionaries, a Christian education.

Mr. Butscher having spent some time in England, having recruited his health, married a wife in every way qualified to assist him in his work, and received the parting instructions of the Committee, prepared to return to Africa with his new associates. He embarked on board the brig "Charles," Captain Graham, on the 19th of November, 1812. Early in the month of January, 1813, the ship made Cape de Verde, and shortly after passed the island of Goree.* The weather was fine, and the missionaries expected to enter the Rio Pongas in a few days; but "he who measureth the waters in the hollow of his hand" had decided otherwise. At eleven o'clock on the night of the 5th of January, the "Charles" struck on a reef of rocks about five miles from the coast. Most of the passengers were asleep in their berths, but the violence with which the vessel struck, roused them, and they rushed on deck. It appeared at first that the vessel, with all

* Goree is a small island, about a mile to the south of Cape de Verde. The Dutch were the first Europeans who took possession of it. They called it Goree, after a small island near the mouth of the Maese. The French took it from the Dutch, but surrendered it to the British in 1800. It was re-taken in 1804 by the French, who, however, were again soon compelled to surrender it; but it was finally restored to them in 1816, when, by the Treaty of Vienna, the balance of power was adjusted amongst the great nations of Europe.

on board, must be lost; and in the prospect of approaching death, Mr. Butscher did his duty as a faithful minister, and exhorted all on board "to commit their souls into the hands of a compassionate and forgiving Saviour."

Contrary to all expectation, however, the vessel held together till morning, when it was discovered that, if lightened, she might float, and be got off the reef; but every effort to get her off failed, and the pumps were kept continually going, to prevent her from falling and sinking in the deep water. On the morning of the 11th, Mr. Butscher volunteered to go in one of the boats to Goree for assistance. He went, accompanied by his wife, Mr. and Mrs. Quast, and his African *protégé*, Richard Wilkinson. For five days they were tossed about by contrary winds, in a stormy sea, and at last, on the 16th, they reached Goree.

Having obtained the assistance of Captain Gibson, who commanded the brig "Neptune," Mr. Butscher left his wife and companions at Goree, and returned with Captain Gibson to the wreck of the "Charles." What was his surprise and horror to find that, during his absence, Captain Graham and one of the passengers had been brutally murdered by a party of natives, and that the rest of the passengers with the crew had fled in boats to Goree. It was found impossible to save the cargo of the "Charles," which was seized by the savages, and Mr.

Butscher returned to Goree to rejoin his companions, who had begun to fear that he had fallen into the hands of the murderers of Captain Graham.

The wreck of the "Charles" proved a serious blow to the missionaries. They had taken with them from England large supplies of necessaries for the use of themselves and their brethren at the settlement. Provisions, wearing apparel, materials for building, tools, books—all were lost. Even the few articles of personal property which Mr. Butscher had contrived to save, and bring with him to Goree, were sold for the benefit of the underwriters, as he had taken the precaution to insure everything he possessed before leaving England. "I kept, however," he says, "two good old suits of clothes till the auction commenced, which, I think. was more than the apostle Paul retained when he suffered shipwreck."

Whilst the missionaries were detained at Goree, exactly one month after the wreck of the "Charles," Mrs. Meyer, the wife of the rope-maker, was taken ill, and in three days died; so that, although they had escaped the dangers of the sea, they had no security against the still greater danger of the African climate.

The commandant at Goree, Major Chisholm, proved to the missionary party a true friend. Seeing how they were circumstanced, and knowing their anxiety to re-purchase some of the things which were to be sold by auction, he, together with Lieutenant Colonel McCarthy, Governor of Senegal, advanced to them, on the Society's account, upwards of £500; and this enabled them to obtain many things which were absolutely necessary to enable them to settle at the Rio Pongas. Two months were spent in Goree; and on the 2nd of March they left in a Spanish ship for the settlement, where their brethren had been diligently labouring in their absence. During the voyage, John Quast, the boat-builder, was attacked by fever, and died just one hour before the vessel came to an anchor at the Rio Pongas. Mr. and Mrs. Renner came down to welcome their friends, and were not a little startled to find that one of them had just breathed his last. The surviving missionaries came on shore, and nearly the whole night was spent in conversation on the strange and sad events that had occurred during the fifteen months that they had been separated. John Quast's remains were committed to the earth by Mr. Renner; and after Mr. Butscher had placed his surviving companions under the care of Mr. and Mrs. Renner, he and his wife proceeded to Sierra Leone.

For some months past, the colony had been left without a chaplain, Mr. Nyländer having gone off on a mission to the Bulloms. The Committee had therefore authorized Mr. Butscher to discharge the duties of chaplain if he obtained the permission of the Governor. He was at the same time required to act as the Society's missionary to the heathen in the colony; he was to superintend the missionary schools, and to be the medium of communication between the secretaries in London and the brethren labouring at the Rio Pongas. All these duties Mr. Butscher discharged with exemplary zeal and diligence.

So far, missionary work in Africa had been only in its infancy. Nine years had elapsed since the first missionaries landed on the continent, and very little had been done for the spread of the religion of Jesus Christ amongst the adult population. Many children had been brought under Christian instruction, but neither amongst children, nor amongst adults, had there been a single case of what might be regarded as genuine conversion from heathenism. The Church Missionary Society had hitherto devoted its time and its energies rather to the instruction of the young than to the evangelization of the adult population. But now a change was made. Instructions were sent out to the missionaries in 1814, and the first was that—" Public worship and the preaching of the gospel are to be maintained every Sunday in each settlement, in a building appropriated to that object; and the natives who understand the language sufficiently, are to be invited and urged to attend." Each missionary was required to keep prominently in view these three objects:—1st. By his example to exhibit to all, the happy influences of Christianity on the conduct. 2ndly. To afford Christian instruction to all children in the schools. 3rdly. To proclaim the "glad tidings of salvation" to all around.

When Mr. Butscher was directed by the Committee of the Church Missionary Society to fill the office of chaplain at Sierra Leone, he felt great difficulty in making up his mind to do so. The great object on which he had set his heart was the formation of a settlement on the river Dembia, to be called the Gambier Settlement, in honour of Admiral Lord Gambier, the first President of the Society. He considered that to accept the office of chaplain would be virtually to abandon his missionary work. When, on the other hand, he considered that there were ten thousand souls in the colony, amongst whom there were many heathen, and that it was of the utmost importance, not only to the Europeans, but also to the natives, to have a Christian minister resident amongst them, he consented to remain in Sierra Leone, without, however, abandoning altogether his intention of forming the Gambier settlement.

The revival of the slave trade on the Rio Pongas, caused Mr. Butscher much anxiety. In six months about a thousand of the natives were carried off, and sold as slaves. Death, too, was busy amongst the small missionary band. Herman Meyer, whose wife had died at Goree, expired on the 12th September, just six months after his arrival at Bassia.

These misfortunes were, however, relieved, by the occurrence of a most interesting event. On the 20th of January, 1814, the foundation stone of the first Christian church that had ever been seen in that part of Africa was laid at Bassia. Four African boys were selected to perform the mason's part in laying the stone. Mr. Renner conducted the religious part of the services; the blessing of God was solemnly invoked, and as soon as the assembly had dispersed the workmen took possession of the place and commenced their labours. Mr. Wilhelm, after giving an account of the day's proceedings, adds the following prayer, to which every faithful Christian will heartily say "Amen."—" May it please God to forward, accomplish, and uphold this building with his Almighty hand, as his holy temple in the midst of devils' houses and abominable places of idolatry; and may the constant sounding of the glorious gospel in this house of God cause the Sun of Righteousness to arise and shine amongst those habitations of darkness and cruelty, so as to make them vanish like vapours on the rising of the sun."

A month later, on the 20th of February, 1814, the foundation of a second church was laid at Canoffee; and both churches were, by dint of great exertions, covered in before the rainy season commenced.

CHAPTER IV.

FIRST DROPS OF THE SHOWER OF BLESSING.

"So shall he sprinkle many nations."—ISAIAH lii, 15.

WHILST the building of the churches mentioned in the last chapter was progressing, a great misfortune befel the settlement at Canoffee.

A body of black soldiers from Sierra Leone, under the command of two English officers, had been sent into the interior to check, or if possible, suppress the slave trade, which had, during the few months preceding, been revived, with the connivance of some of the chiefs. Some of the factories of the slave dealers had been destroyed by the soldiers, upon which the dealers resolved to wreak their vengeance on the missionaries, at whose instigation, they supposed, the soldiers had come into the country. Nothing prevented the immediate execution of their diabolical plans, except the fear of exasperating some of the powerful chiefs, whose children were receiving a good education at the mission schools. They waited, however, at Bassia, for an opportunity to carry out their designs, and it being well known that mischief was intended, the missionaries, both at Bassia and Canoffee, felt considerable alarm. Matters continued in this state until the 11th of April, when a slave dealer, whose house had been destroyed by the military, set fire in revenge to a field of dry grass near the settlement. The grass at that season was very combustible, and the fire rapidly approached Canoffee. The house in which Mr. and Mrs. Meissner lived was burned to the ground, and nearly everything belonging to them was destroyed.

It can hardly be wondered at, that under these circumstances, the missionaries should have begun to feel doubts about the permanence of their position. The Colonial Government could not do otherwise than punish men who were setting all law, human and divine, at defiance; and so long as the slave traders were pursued by a military force, and kept in subjection by the power of the sword, they would endeavour to inflict injury on the missionaries, whom they believed to be the only obstacle in the way of the full development of the slave trade. The prospect of a removal was now severely felt, as the two churches were nearly completed, and it was hoped that within their walls the Gospel of Jesus Christ would be fully and faithfully preached amongst the people who had hitherto heard only a faint utterance of its glorious truths.

In the midst of these calamities the missionaries were again attacked by illness. Both Mr. Renner and Mr. Wilhelm suffered much from the African fever. One of the children in the school died. Conrad Meissner, the smith, also fell a victim to the climate; and Mrs. Quast, the boat-builder's widow, who had obtained leave to go to England for the recovery of her health, died on the voyage. The little band was now greatly reduced in numbers; but the faith and zeal of those who remained were as ardent as ever. Shortly after the destruction of Mr. Meissner's house by fire, it was feared that it would be necessary to abandon the settlement altogether; but the thought was dismissed as one unworthy of those who had been called to "endure hardness as good soldiers of Jesus Christ;" and the survivors of this little missionary army remained bravely at their post, contending manfully with heathen superstition, and "not counting their lives dear unto them so that they might finish their course with joy and the ministry which they had received of the Lord Jesus, to testify the gospel of the grace of God."

Mr. Butscher had resolved, as I have already said, to form a settlement on the river Dembia, to which the name of Gambier should be given. Accordingly, early in the year 1814, he selected a suitable place on that river, and there, a piece of land having been purchased, a house was erected upon it, and preparations were made for opening a school. The settlement was thenceforth called the Gambier Settlement, and placed under the care of Mr. and Mrs. Klein.

Whilst the mission to the Soosoos was, as I have shown, beset with dangers, which at one time threatened to lead to its complete extinction, that to the Bulloms was prospering. Mr. Nyländer had been labouring diligently, not only to instruct the children, but to preach to the adult portion of the population. The place where he erected his missionary settlement was called Yongroo Pomoh, or Little Yongroo. Amongst the Bulloms were many Mohammedans, to whom Mr. Nyländer gave copies of the Bible in the Arabic language. One of the copies he gave to the Bullom king, who was so pleased with its contents that he earnestly recommended it to the strangers who came to visit him; and on one occasion Mr. Nyländer, having gone to pay his respects to the king, found about twenty learned Mohammedans seated around him, one of whom, a man advanced in years, was reading to them "the white man's book." This same old man afterwards went to Mr. Nyländer and asked for a copy of the book, which was gladly given to him. He seemed pretty well acquainted with the contents of the New Testament, and indeed every Mohammedan to whom passages out of the New Testament were read, expressed very great admiration of it.

It has already been stated that the Church Missionary Society had determined to adopt the plan of redeeming as many African children as possible from slavery, this being, at the time of which I am writing, the only available way of rescuing them from that terrible condition. As, however, great exertions were, from time to time, made by the Government to suppress the slave trade, and as many thousands of Africans were rescued from the slave ships and landed at Sierra Leone, the Committee of the Church Missionary Society resolved to carry out another plan. The children of the liberated Africans were formally adopted by the Society, and a fund was set on foot for the maintenance and education of these children. To this fund liberal contributions were made; and in their Fifteenth Annual Report, the Committee announced that the sum received then amounted to £500, which at a cost of £5 per head would maintain 100 children. These children received, as was natural, the names of their English friends and benefactors; and accordingly, when we read the annals of the West African Church, we find the swarthy sons of Africa bearing such honoured names as Claudius Buchanan, Henry Martyn, Josiah Pratt, Thomas Scott, Charles Simeon, Daniel Wilson, with many others. A great many girls, too, were named after English ladies, who devoted much of their time and attention to the

G

temporal and spiritual welfare of the women of Sierra Leone.

The Church Missionary Society now began to direct its attention to the establishment of institutions under the protection of the British Government, in the places most favourable to the diffusion of Christianity amongst the heathen. A grant of land having been made to the Society in Sierra Leone, it was determined that the first experiment of this kind should be tried in that colony. "These institutions" the Committee said in their Fifteenth Annual Report, "will serve as points of support to the exertions of the Society in their respective quarters; they may be rendered the asylums of the widows and orphans, and they will become in various ways the source of beneficent influence over the surrounding tribes. The Society have already four settlements on the coast of Africa, in which 200 native children receive Christian instruction. These settlements are subject to the caprice of the natives; but the institutions in question will be secure under the protection of the Colonial Government of Sierra Leone."

In November 1814, the Society sent forth more labourers to Western Africa. These were the Rev. John Christopher Sperrhacken and his wife; Mr. and Mrs. Hughes; Jellorum Harrison and Thomas Morgan, Africans who had been educated in England; and Mrs. Hartwig, wife of the Missionary who, as has been stated, had been dismissed from the service of the Society in 1807.*

After a prosperous voyage, the new band of Missionaries arrived in Sierra Leone on the 13th of February, 1815, and were warmly welcomed by Mr. and Mrs. Butscher and their companions. It was arranged that Mr. Hughes should at once enter on his duties as schoolmaster, and that Mr. and Mrs. Sperrhacken should join Mr. Nyländer's mission amongst the Bulloms. The Africans were to be made useful as opportunities for employing them arose, and Mrs. Hartwig was to join her husband who, however, died shortly afterwards, as recorded in the subjoined note.

The contemplated restoration of Goree and Senegal to France about this time, revived the

* Mr. Hartwig after his dismissal had wandered about for seven years amongst the neighbouring tribes, and being exposed to many hardships and privations, had been brought by suffering, to feel remorse for his past conduct, and to express an earnest desire to be re-admitted to the position which he had formerly disgraced. The Committee, whilst they had every reason to believe his repentance to be sincere, did not approve of his being again employed as a Missionary, until by a course of consistent conduct he had re-established his character amongst the Africans, but they agreed to employ him as an interpreter and translator during good behaviour. He remained in the service of the Society in this capacity only a few months. In the month of March, 1815, death put an end to his career. His wife had for some years supported herself by honest labour in England; but hearing of her husband's amendment of life she thought it her duty to return to Africa and to him; and accordingly she was allowed by the Committee to join the party that left England towards the close of the year 1814.

hopes of the Soosoo chiefs that the slave trade would be re-established in full vigour by the French; and numerous meetings were held by them to decide on the best means of protecting the trade. One of these meetings was held on the 5th of December, 1814; and the resolution to which the assembled chiefs came, was, that they would defend themselves against their enemies "both those to the north and those to the south," meaning the Foulahs and the British. Under the apprehension in England of a revival of the French slave trade, 864 petitions were presented to Parliament, signed by 8000 persons, invoking the exertion of British influence for the suppression of the trade; and Lord Castlereagh obtained from Louis XVIII. a promise that France would at once abolish it.

Disaster now fell upon the missionaries. The settlement at Canoffee was attacked by some of the natives, the plantations which had begun to flourish were laid waste, and all the crops were destroyed. Not content with this, the natives proceeded to Bassia, set fire to the mission buildings, risking the lives of all the inmates, and scattered ruin and desolation all around.

There was no doubt on the minds of the missionaries that these atrocious acts were committed at the instigation of a slave dealer who had publicly threatened to destroy both Bassia and Canoffee. Mr. Renner immediately started for Sierra Leone to consult his friends as to what ought to be done in this emergency. A meeting was held at Freetown, and it was resolved that the buildings at Bassia should be restored, and that neither Bassia nor Canoffee should be abandoned.

More deaths shortly afterwards occurred amongst the devoted band. In April, 1815, Mrs. Hartwig died of yellow fever, and shortly after Mrs. Butscher followed her. The character of the latter stood very high in the colony. She is spoken of as "a woman of acute understanding, considerable attainments, and tried piety."

"Poor Africa!" says Mr. Walker in his account of missions in Western Africa, "her children groan in chains of darkness, and she has nothing to offer those who would draw near to remove them but a grave. Surely none but heavenly fires could burn in the breasts of those who would press forward to perform such a service for such a reward."

We have now arrived at a very important epoch in the history of missionary work in Sierra Leone —the visit of the Rev. Edward Bickersteth in the year 1816.

The affairs of the West African Mission had arrived at a crisis when it was absolutely necessary that some decisive step should be taken by the Committee, either to place the settlements outside the colony on some more secure basis than the caprice of slave dealers, or else to abandon them altogether, and carry on their work within the limits of the colony where they were sure of protection. They were, however, desirous before they took any important step, to be fully informed as to the actual state of affairs in Africa; and they resolved to send thither some friend of the Society in whom they could repose entire confidence, that he might examine into every part of its concerns, and there obtain accurate information, apply a present remedy to any evils that might have arisen, form on the spot his own judgment in respect of future proceedings, and return to assist by his counsel the deliberations of the Committee. Such a friend was happily found in the Rev. Edward Bickersteth, to whose exertions the Church Missionary Society had already been largely indebted. Mr. Pratt thus announced the event to his brethren in Africa. "An excellent and able friend of the Society, Mr. Bickersteth, of Norwich, is about to be ordained. He will then sail for Sierra Leone as the Society's visitor."

Mr. Bickersteth left England on the 24th of January, 1816, and after spending three months in Africa, reached home on the 18th of August. I may here mention, even though I travel a little out of the order of the narrative, that on the 13th of September a deputation of the Church Missionary Society waited on the Government to propose various arrangements suggested by the information which

Mr. Bickersteth had collected, and by the plans and representations of the Governor of Sierra Leone. Amongst these arrangements it was proposed to divide the colony into parishes, and to increase the number of English clergymen and schoolmasters, for the effectual care and instruction of the re-captured negroes. The Government fully concurred in these plans. The division speedily took place; and assistance was given to the Church Missionary Society by a share of the salaries of the missionaries being defrayed from the public treasury.

The mission on which Mr. Bickersteth left his native country was an important and a responsible one. Nearly twelve years had passed away since the Society had sent its first missionaries to the coast of Africa. These years had been years of trial and disappointment. It pleased God that in Africa, as elsewhere, his servants should sow in tears before they were permitted to reap in joy. Many who had been sent into the mission field had fallen victims to the deadly climate, and no remarkable success had attended the efforts of those who were left. The natives, whose only intercourse with Europeans had hitherto been through the medium of the slave traders, were completely debased by its pernicious influence. They desired nothing but money from the missionaries who came to give them instruction. These discouragements, added to the difficulty of acquiring the native languages and the dangers arising from the climate, had so disheartened the missionaries that they had almost given up preaching to the adults and had given their chief attention to the schools in the settlements. They had thus neglected the chief object for which the Society was formed. That object was to declare to the heathen, by means of preaching, the gospel of the grace of God. At the schools the children were wholly removed from their heathen parents, and clothed and boarded at the expense of the Society. Many of them made great progress in their education, and the schools were justly regarded as green spots in the desert land around. But the management of them was attended with much difficulty. The missionaries having so large a number of children to provide for were necessarily entangled with "the cares of this life;" and without a great deal of watchfulness and prudence on their part, they were liable to incur heavy and needless expense. Some system of supervision was necessary to protect the Society against the errors of judgment into which any individual missionary was liable to fall. Besides all this, circumstances had greatly changed since the first establishment of the mission. Then, as we have already seen, the Soosoos seemed to offer the most promising field for missionary exertion. Since that time, the colony of Sierra Leone had risen in importance; captured slave ships were continually bringing in cargoes of natives from all parts of the coast, and the Governor was anxious that the strength of the mission should be directed to this point, where so many heathen were already assembled under British protection. All these circumstances made it desirable that a visitor from England should inspect the mission; but it was rendered imperative (alas! that we should have to confess it) by the fact that dissensions had arisen amongst the missionaries, and accusations had been made against some of them which it was absolutely necessary to investigate on the spot.

Mr. Bickersteth's instructions were to converse privately with all connected with the mission, to assemble them together if he judged it expedient, in order to discuss with them matters of importance, and also to obtain all the information he could from heathen chiefs, and from any person resident in the colony or settlements, about the disputes which had arisen. He was to ascertain the character of the missionaries, their manner of carrying on their work, the influence they exercised, the progress made in the schools, and the number of schoolmasters required in the colony. He had authority, if he judged it requisite, to suspend or remove any one connected with the mission. "He was," in the words of his instructions, "to strengthen the weak, to comfort the dejected, to endeavour to become all things to all men." He felt very deeply the responsibility of an office which demanded of him so much firmness, tenderness, and wisdom in dealing with the missionaries, and so much prudence and judgment in dealing with the details of the work entrusted to them. His journal will be found quoted at length in Mr. Walker's "Church Missions in Western Africa."

On the 22nd of February, 1816, Mr. Bickersteth arrived at Goree, and on the 7th of March, at Sierra Leone. He remained only a week in the colony, being anxious to visit the settlements on the Rio Pongas. From Governor McCarthy, Mr. Bickersteth received the greatest attention. He was disposed to concur in the Governor's opinion, that the main efforts of the Society should be directed to the welfare of the liberated slaves in the colony. "It appears," he wrote in his journal, "very important to mark the indications of a providential leading. Among these, I consider, the protection of an established government, the facility and safety of intercourse with the people, the economy attending a mission, and the number that may be easily gathered together. In the absence of supernatural inspiration, such circumstances may be considered as the call, 'Come over and help us,' and all these things speak strongly in favour of our exertions in the colony."

In the middle of March, Mr. Bickersteth, accompanied by Mr. Nyländer, started for the Rio Pongas. They visited first the Gambier settlement at Kapparoo, and spent a week there. Towards the end of the month, they arrived at Bassia.* Mr. Bickersteth's decision, after a careful inspection of the Bassia settlement, was, that it ought to be abandoned, and all the children removed to Canoffee, which afforded greater facilities for carrying on both educational and missionary work than Bassia.

On inquiry, he found that no part of the conduct of the missionaries had given any offence to the natives. They possessed, to the fullest extent, the confidence both of the chiefs and the people. But amongst the missionaries themselves, there existed disunion and discord, arising, in a great measure, from jealousy. On this subject, Mr. Bickersteth spoke to them as follows:—"I feel obliged to notice that disunion which our great enemy has excited amongst you. Be assured this is a most serious obstacle to the success of the mission which you have at heart. * * * * I have endeavoured carefully to examine into the grounds of the disunion that has arisen. You have each, I believe, candidly opened your minds to me on the subject. Some of these grounds have been mere mis-information and mistake. Some have been such, that I have been really utterly ashamed, sometimes that

* Mr. Bickersteth examined the children in the school at Bassia, and in his report, expressed his great gratification at what he saw and heard. "No English school that I am acquainted with," he said, "would have answered the questions so seriously and so feelingly."

such needless cause of offence should have been hastily given by one, and sometimes that offence should so unnecessarily have been taken by another. None, however, affect, as far as I can at present judge, the sincerity of the Christian character. I see no reason, therefore, whatever, why each should not, from this moment, lay aside all distance, distrust, and suspicion, and unite and act together for the future in love."

This faithful and Christian remonstrance was not without good results on those to whom it was addressed.

On the 16th of April, Mr. Bickersteth having finished his work at the settlement, set sail to return to Sierra Leone, which he reached on the 20th of that month.

Whilst at Sierra Leone, his attention was much occupied with the Christian Institution at Leicester Mountain. About 300 African children were assembled there. They were maintained partly by Government, and partly by the benefactions of private individuals; and after receiving some preparatory education, they were apprenticed to mechanics and tradesmen, and trained to become useful members of society.

From Sierra Leone, Mr. Bickersteth crossed the river to visit the Yongroo Pomoh settlement, on the Bullom shore. There he witnessed scenes of heathenism so terrible, that they made on him an impression which was never effaced. His time was occupied, much as it had been at Bassia and Canoffee, in examining the school children, and visiting the native villages. On the 2nd of May, he was compelled to return to Sierra Leone, by the tidings that a vessel, the "Echo," had arrived, bringing out four new schoolmasters, with their wives, to whom he was required to assign posts. Amongst these schoolmasters was Mr. Johnson, who was afterwards ordained, and who became one of the most successful missionaries ever employed by the Society in Africa.

In the beginning of June, 1816, Mr. Bickersteth's work in Africa was almost completed. The instructions given to him had been diligently carried out. He had bestowed particular attention on the examination of the children in the schools; he had made minute inquiries into every matter affecting the welfare of the mission, not neglecting even the smallest details of household economy; he had laboured to remove impediments in the way of preaching the gospel to the heathen, and had himself set a good example as a preacher. He had diligently exercised his ministry in the colony, and in the delicate task of settling differences amongst his brethren, had striven patiently to examine into the causes of dissension, to elicit the truth, to restore those who had fallen, and to place each where his talents would be most useful, and where he would be least exposed to temptation.

Many pleasing testimonies were borne to the value of Mr. Bickersteth's labours in Africa. Amongst others, Governor McCarthy thus referred to his exertions in a letter to Earl Bathurst :—" Mr. Bickersteth remained only a short period here, but I form the most sanguine expectations that his meritorious zeal and exertions will prove highly conducive to the important objects which brought him to the Coast; and I refer with pleasure to that gentleman for such more minute information as your Lordship may wish to obtain relating to this part of His Majesty's dominions."

To Mr. Bickersteth himself the Governor wrote under date February 5th, 1817 :—" I am happy to say that everything is at present going on very prosperously, and should you be inclined to sacrifice your comfort again in two or three years, and come and see the fruits of the trees which, if you did not plant, you fostered and preserved from destruction, I have no doubt that you would be much and amply gratified."

Sailing in the "Echo," on the 7th of June, 1816, for Barbadoes, Mr. Bickersteth reached home, as already stated, on the 18th of August.*

---

* The instructions given by the Committee to Mr. Bickersteth, with his reply, will be found in the Sixteenth Annual Report of the Church Missionary Society; and in the Appendix to that Report will be found Mr. Bickersteth's account of his visit to Africa, with suggestions for the future management of the mission, and recommendations relating to expenditure, superintendence, and visitation.

During the first six months of the year 1816, six individuals connected with the mission died, amongst whom was Mr. Sperrhacken. The four schoolmasters, with their wives, who had arrived in the "Echo," were intended to supply the vacancies caused by death.

The Society's Reports at the time of which I am now writing, contain melancholy details of deaths amongst the heroic band of missionaries. Even Mr. Butscher, who was supposed to have become thoroughly acclimatized, at last fell a victim to the climate. For nearly eleven years he had laboured with great zeal and judgment amidst formidable difficulties of all kinds, and just as he was beginning to see some of the fruits of his toil, his earthly pilgrimage came to a close. The country fever cut him down; and on the 17th of July, 1817, his remains were consigned to "the white man's grave."

I have already said that after the Bassia settlement had, on Mr. Bickersteth's recommendation been given up, the children under training and the movable property of the Society were transferred to Canoffee. In February, 1818, it was found impossible to retain this position. The slave trade with all its horrors was revived, and neither life nor property was safe for one moment at Canoffee. It took three months to make arrangements for a move; and on the 21st of May, Mr. and Mrs. Renner, accompanied by sixty children—forty more having been sent home at the request of their parents—abandoned their last stronghold at Canoffee, and retired to Sierra Leone, where they might live in safety under the protection of the British flag.

It must not be supposed that the labour expended on Bassia and Canoffee had been expended in vain. Nearly four hundred heathen children had received from the missionaries a Christian education, and from kind friends in England food and clothing, whilst not a few adult Africans had had the gospel of the Saviour preached to them in all its fulness. At the time of the departure from Canoffee, the number of children who had been plucked from heathenism and brought under Christian influences amounted to three hundred and ninety-three.

The Gambier and Bullom settlements were still maintained, notwithstanding the difficulties arising from the existence of the slave trade. Of these outposts, however, I shall not now speak. I wish rather to direct the attention of the reader to the rapid progress of Christianity and its accompanying civilization within the limits of the colony of Sierra Leone.

With the appointment of Mr Johnson, who, as has been already related, arrived in the spring of 1816, a new era seems to have commenced in the history of the colony.

William Augustine Bernard Johnson was a native of Hanover, and by trade a sugar refiner. When twenty-eight years of age he offered himself as a schoolmaster, and his wife as a schoolmistress, to the Committee of the Church Missionary Society. His offer was, after very careful deliberation, accepted, and Sierra Leone was assigned to him as the scene of his labours.

In the month of June, 1816, Mr. Johnson entered on his duties. On the 14th of that month, in view of the work allotted to him amongst the liberated negroes, Mr. Johnson wrote these words in his journal:—"Oh! how I have been cast down this day. If I ever have seen wretchedness it has been to-day. I was told that six or seven died in one day. These poor people may indeed be called the offscouring of Africa. But shall I despair now? No. The first shall be last, and the last first. Who knows whether the Lord will not make his converting power known among these poor depraved people. With Him nothing is impossible."

Mr. Johnson did not despair. For three years he toiled unremittingly and hopefully, and the change which was effected during those three years was so remarkable, that the opponents of missionary work amongst the negroes were completely staggered, and the friends and supporters of the work were encouraged to go on, in dependence on the promise of the Great Head of the Church—"Lo! I am with you always."

In March, 1817, at the express wish of the Com-

H

mittee, Mr. Johnson was ordained by his brethren Renner, Butscher, and Wenzel, according to the forms of the Lutheran Church, and after this date he diligently assisted in conducting the public services of the mission without in any way neglecting his special work, the education of the young.

The Twentieth Report of the Church Missionary Society furnishes us with details of Mr. Johnson's work during the three years which elapsed between his arrival at Sierra Leone in 1816 and his first visit to England in 1819. No one who reads that report, the accuracy of which cannot be doubted, can hesitate to confess that the history of the Christian Church has never afforded a more striking instance of the power of the gospel in civilizing and blessing savage man.

When large numbers of negroes were brought together in Sierra Leone in the year 1813, they were found to be in a most deplorable condition. In 1816 Mr. Bickersteth, as above related, visited the colony and found about eleven hundred liberated negroes under the care of the colonial authorities. They consisted of persons taken from almost all the tribes in that part of the African continent. The efforts of those who had charge of them, under the vigilant and anxious inspection of the Governor, had greatly improved the condition of those who had resided there for some time. Every measure that it was possible to adopt in order to accomplish this end had been adopted by the Governor; and a church had been erected in anticipation of the regular establishment of Christian worship amongst the natives. The Governor felt that a powerful stimulus was required to rouse the negroes to diligence; and that an energetic principle was wanted which might harmonize their jarring feelings and unite them as one body. That stimulus was found in the sense of duty and of gratitude which Christianity inspires; and that uniting principle in the healing spirit of the gospel of Jesus Christ.

At the desire of the Governor, Mr. Johnson was appointed to take spiritual charge of the negroes living at Regent's Town. Natives belonging to twenty-two different nations were here collected together, and a considerable number of them had been but recently liberated from the holds of slave vessels. They were greatly prejudiced against one another, and in a state of continual hostility, with no common medium of intercourse but a little broken English. When clothing was given to them they sold it or threw it away. It was very difficult to induce them to put it on; and it was found quite impossible to persuade them to wear it constantly until an example had been set by Mr. Johnson's servant girl. The tie of marriage was, apparently, unknown amongst them; and there did not seem to be any restraint placed on the union of the opposite sexes. In some huts ten of them were crowded together; and in others fifteen or twenty. Many of them were reduced to the condition of skeletons. Six or eight frequently died in one day, and only six infants were born during the year. Superstition in various forms tyrannized over them. Many built devil's houses, and all wore "gregrees" or charms. Scarcely any desire for improvement was discernible. For a long time there were hardly ever more than five or six acres of land under cultivation; and some who wished to cultivate the soil, were deterred from doing so by the fear of being robbed of the produce. Some lived in the woods away from all society; others subsisted by stealing fowls, ducks, and pigs, from any who possessed them. During the first week of his residence amongst them, Mr. Johnson had thirty fowls stolen from him. They would eat fowls and ducks raw, and not a few of them, particularly those of the Ebo nation, the most savage of all, preferred any kind of refuse to the excellent rations served out to them by the Government.

The improvement in the whole of these liberated negroes was in a few years very marked: and it was an improvement brought about, not by an appeal to the selfish feelings of their nature, or by holding out to them any worldly inducements to abandon evil practices. It was the act of that same Divine Power which, centuries ago, produced, by the same Divine Truth, a mighty change in our own barbarous ancestors, which softened their ferocious natures, which stripped the skins of beasts and cleansed the savage daubings from their persons, which stanched the blood of human victims, exposed to shame the cruelties of their Pagan idolatry, and gave birth to those laws and institutions which have made us the greatest amongst the nations of the earth.

In three years the town was enlarged, by the formation of nineteen new streets. A large church was erected. A Government House, a parsonage, hospital, school-house, besides store-houses, a bridge, and rows of dwelling-houses, all built of stone, arose as if by magic. Gardens were fenced in; all the available land was placed under cultivation; cassadas, plaintains, yams, coffee, and Indian corn were grown; bananas, oranges, limes, pine-apples, ground-nuts, guavas, and other kinds of fruit, were carefully cultivated; and horses, cows, bullocks, sheep, goats, pigs, ducks, hens, and other animals, were possessed by the inhabitants of Regent's Town. A daily market was held, and on Saturdays this market was attended by very large numbers. Nearly all the people understood something of farming, but many who were farmers, followed other occupations as well. There were masons, bricklayers, carpenters, sawyers, tailors, blacksmiths, and butchers. In these different ways upwards of six hundred negroes maintained themselves, and were enabled, in the short space of four or five years, by the fruits of their own productive industry, to relieve from all expense, on their personal account, the Government, to which they paid the most grateful allegiance.

In appearance and manners the improvement was not less marked. The people learned to wear decent clothing. Almost all the women made their own clothes. About four hundred couples were married. The dancing and drumming, in which, as heathens, they used sometimes to spend whole nights, ceased. In six months only six deaths occurred in the town; whilst, in three months, forty-two children were born. An oath was never heard in the town, and drunkenness was rarely seen. The attendance on public worship was regular and large. On an average, the number present was twelve hundred. Mr. Johnson's first congregation at Regent's Town consisted of only nine persons. At morning and evening daily prayers, not less than five hundred were present, after the lapse of four years: and the schools which, when they were opened, contained ninety-six boys, with fifty girls, and thirty-six adults, in four years contained upwards of five hundred pupils of all ages.

These were great encouragements to Mr. Johnson, but he was not satisfied with a reformation which was merely external. He was anxious to see the influence of the Divine Spirit exerting itself on the hearts of the people confided to his care, and rendering their religion a heartfelt religion, acceptable to God through Jesus Christ. Nor was he disappointed. Many became pious and humble Christians, and manifested, not merely in words, but in their daily lives, the influence of genuine religion. When Mr. Johnson left Regent's Town, for a visit to England, in 1819, the number of communicants amounted to two hundred and sixty-three.

Mr. Jesty, who visited Regent's Town in the month of April, 1819, thus records his impression of what he saw on Sunday:—"At ten o'clock I saw a sight which at once astonished and delighted me. The bell at the church was rung for divine service, on which Mr. Johnson's well-regulated schools of boys and girls walked two and two to the church. The eagerness of the inhabitants to hear the Word will appear from their early attendance on the means of grace. It is true that there is a bell in the steeple of the church, but it is of little use at Regent's Town, for the church is generally filled half an hour before the bell tolls. The greatest attention is paid during the service. Indeed, I witnessed a Christian congregation in a heathen land—a people fearing God and working righteousness. The tear of godly sorrow rolled down many a coloured cheek, and shewed the contrition of a heart that felt its own vileness.

"At three o'clock in the afternoon there was again a very full attendance, so that scarcely an individual was to be seen throughout the town; so eager are they to hear the Word, and feed on that living bread that came down from heaven.

"At six we met again; and although many had to come from a considerable distance, and up a tremendous hill, I did not perceive any decrease of number, or weariness in their attendance on the means of grace. Never did I witness such a congregation in a professing Christian land, nor ever behold such apparent sincerity and brotherly love."

I have already said that Mr. Johnson found it necessary to pay a short visit to England in the year 1819. The circumstances connected with his departure were very interesting. An extract from his journal, dated Easter Sunday, April 11th, will show what rapid progress had been made in the missionary work at Regent's Town. "The church," he says, "was full at nine o'clock. I married two couples, baptized a hundred and ten adults, and six infants, and administered the Lord's Supper to two hundred and fifty-three black brethren and sisters, and four whites, with myself making up two hundred and fifty-eight. This was as a day of Pentecost in Africa."

A few days after Mr. Johnson's faithful negroes

accompanied him to Freetown, and took their leave of him for a time. Hundreds of both sexes, and of various ages, assembled to say farewell, with many tears. In their ardent affection for the earnest pastor who had been the means of bringing them out of the wilderness of heathenism into the fold of Christ, they expressed their regret that they could not be the companions of his voyage; and they dismissed him from their shores with their warm benedictions, and a simple but striking utterance of their love—"Massa, suppose no water live here," pointing to the sea, "we go with you all the way till no feet more."

A great experiment had been tried, and it had been successful.

When Benjamin Franklin flew his kite tipped with iron in order to prove the identity of lightning with the electric fluid, he watched patiently, with uplifted eyes, the passing of a dense cloud which heralded the storm; and when, a few minutes afterwards great drops of rain fell and with them the lightning ran along the string of his kite and reached the ground, Franklin breathed freely, for he knew that a wonderful discovery had been made. The drops of rain were succeeded by an abundant shower, the single stream of electricity by a constant outpouring of fire from heaven; and a problem that had puzzled many sages was solved.

In Africa too, a few drops of spiritual blessing

had descended upon her swarthy sons. The divine fire of love had passed from heaven to earth, and had kindled a sacred flame in hearts that had been cold with an icy coldness. A great problem had been solved. The philosopher who had ranked the negro with the beasts of the field had been proved to be wrong: the Christian who believed him to be possessed of an immortal soul had been proved to be right. Men could no longer say that the possession of a black skin ought to exclude from the rights of humanity, or from the privileges of the Christian Church. The negro had asserted his humanity in a way that was unmistakable, he had completely demonstrated his brotherhood, he had taken his place in the great family of the Universal Father, he had listened to and had believed the "gospel of the grace of God;" and that gospel by its irresistible influence had raised him from the depths of misery, and had taught him both to rejoice in the life that now is, and to look forward with ever-increasing joy to the life that is to come.

CHAPTER V.

THE LEADERS OF THE FORLORN HOPE.

"Each stepping where his comrade stood
The instant that he fell."—SIR WALTER SCOTT.

IN the month of January, 1820, Mr. Johnson returned to his labours at Regent's Town, accompanied by his wife and sister. Several schoolmasters and schoolmistresses also accompanied him, and in order to decide on the stations which should be allotted to each, a meeting of the whole missionary band was held on the 3rd of February. There were now twenty-eight persons connected with the Society in the colony, and upwards of two thousand pupils were receiving Christian instruction in the Society's schools.

Mr. Johnson had established the Regent's Town Auxiliary of the Church Missionary Society. On the 25th of February, 1820, the second anniversary meeting of the Auxiliary was held, and a new feature in the proceedings was that speeches were made by several of the negroes. The speeches did not possess the elegance or the polish which sometimes marks the speeches delivered at missionary meetings in this Christian land; but they were the utterances of men whose hearts overflowed with gratitude to God for all his goodness. Let one specimen out of many suffice:—"Missionary come here," said the sable speaker, "and preach to us and we pay nothing. England make us free, and bring us to this country. God, my brothers, has done great things for us; but I have denied him like Peter. I can say I am guilty before Him; but He will have mercy upon whom He will have mercy. Oh! may He have mercy upon me. I am not able to do anything. I pray God make us help God's word to cover the earth as the waters cover the sea. I believe that that word will come true. If any got a penny let him give it, and pray God to bless our Society."

There is a freshness about such a speech as this, which we shall seek for in vain in the conventional addresses of many of the speakers on our religious platforms at home. It is nature's eloquence bursting from lips which for centuries had been sealed, but which had, under the influence of the gospel, been opened to proclaim the greatness and the goodness of God; and it affords one proof amongst many, of the marvellous change that had been effected amongst the natives of West Africa in the course of a very few years, by the labours of missionaries.

During the year 1820, rapid progress was made at all the missionary stations in the colony.

Schools sprang up everywhere, congregations were gathered together, order and respect for law prevailed, and the blessings, without the vices, of civilization were introduced. The wilderness had become a fruitful field. Sir George Collier, the Commodore in command of the West African squadron, thus wrote to the Lords of the Admiralty:—"It is hardly possible to conceive the difficulties which have been surmounted in bringing the colony to its present improved and still very improving state. Roads are cut in every direction, useful for communication; many towns and villages are built, and others, as the black population increases, are building; more improvement under all circumstances of climate and infancy of colony is scarcely to be supposed. I visited all the black towns and villages, attended the public schools and other establishments; and I have never witnessed in any population more contentment and happiness. * * * * The manner in which the public schools are here conducted, reflects the greatest credit on those concerned in their prosperity; and the improvement made by the scholars proves the aptitude of the African, if moderate pains be taken to instruct him. I have attended places of public worship in every quarter of the globe, and I do most conscientiously declare that never did I witness the services of religion more piously performed or more devoutly attended to than in Sierra Leone."

The Chief Justice of the colony in a letter to the Committee of the Church Missionary Society, also bore testimony to the devotional demeanour of the negroes in their different village churches, and he congratulated the Society on the successful exertions which had been made to enlighten by the light of the gospel the spiritual darkness of Africa.

The year 1821 opened with the brightest prospects. Life and health had been freely sacrificed in Africa; but the labours and the losses of the devoted band of missionaries were more than requited by the improvement that had been effected. Strange as it may appear to the opponents of missionary work, these once despised Africans became remarkable for their deep, earnest piety, and for their honesty, industry, and docility. Of this statement many striking proofs might be given. Their piety was often manifested in their recognition of the providence of God, in their humble resignation to God's will in times of adversity, and in their fervent expressions of faith in the Divine Redeemer, so different from the formal utterances to which we are accustomed at home. Their honesty was proved on one occasion at least, when a fire broke out at Regent's Town; and although articles of the greatest value lay scattered about for hours, nothing was stolen. Their industry was apparent to every one who visited the colony, and who noticed the neatness of their houses and gardens, and their own personal appearance; and to their docility all those who were placed in authority over them bore ample testimony.

The events of one year were so like those of another, that to enter into minute details of what was done at each missionary station in the colony would be very wearying to the reader. There were few events of a striking or remarkable character. Missionaries and schoolmasters died, and their places were supplied by fresh arrivals from England. Thus the work suffered no interruption.. Everywhere the character of the work was much the same, and was marked by the same signal success.

The question has often been asked—" Ought the teaching of religion to precede or to follow the introduction of civilization into a heathen country?" The history of missionary enterprise in Sierra Leone furnishes an answer to the question. It teaches us that there, at any rate, the precedence of religion was attended by the happiest results. Civilization, if unaccompanied by religion, makes men not better but infinitely worse than they were as savages, by bestowing upon them immense power without any moral principle to control it. If, therefore, civilization precedes religion and acts independently of it, the task of the Christian missionary becomes a hundredfold more difficult; but religion, the pure and holy religion of Christ, which touches the heart, which enlightens the mind, which renovates the character, civilizes, humanizes, softens the whole man, and brings countless blessings in its train.

The Editor of the "Sierra Leone Gazette," at the close of the year 1821, thus expressed his opinion of the effect produced by the labours of missionaries on the population of the colony:—"It is in our liberated African towns that the richest enjoyment awaits the arrival of the philanthropist. There he may contemplate with delight the happy fruits of that system, the primary feature of which is *religious instruction;* and with and proceeding from that instruction, the inculcation of moral and industrious habits, the superiority of the mountain roads, the cleanness and respectable appearance of the villages; but above all, the immense forests cleared away, and the soil covered with the various productions of the climate, fully attest the unremitting industry of these interesting people, while the buildings erected in the respective villages solely by the negroes themselves, mark their capability and improvement as artificers."

The capacity of the Africans for receiving instruction was proved, beyond all doubt, by the missionaries and schoolmasters engaged in teaching them. Mr. Düring, after some years' arduous labour amongst them, wrote as follows:—"Six years' experience has taught me that the African

can learn anything, and that he is not what designing men have represented him, a sort of middle creature, between man and brute. Most of those with whom I live have been brought from the holds of slave ships. I have seen them rise from the chains of the slave-dealer to become industrious men and women, faithful subjects, pious Christians, affectionate husbands and wives, tender fathers and mothers, and peaceable neighbours."

To the improved morals of the people the Chief Justice, the Hon. Edward Fitzgerald, when presiding at the Quarter Sessions, in the year 1822, bore very decided testimony. He observed that ten years before, when the population of the colony was only 4000, there were forty cases on the calendar for trial, and in 1822, when the population had increased to 16,000, there were only *six* cases for trial: so that whilst the population had increased fourfold, the number of criminal cases had been reduced to less than one-sixth. He congratulated the magistrates and the grand jury on the moral improvement of the colony, and remarked with pleasure that there was *not a single case* from any of the villages under the superintendence of a missionary or schoolmaster. The opponents of missionary work will do well, it seems to me, to consider carefully this important fact.

A terrible calamity befel the colony in the summer of 1823. The yellow fever broke out, and swept away many of the military and civilian residents, and some of the missionaries. Three medical men were carried off, and with them a member of the Council, the acting Colonial Secretary, and Chief Justice Fitzgerald.

The death of the Chief Justice was a severe trial to the population, both European and native. He was widely known, and highly esteemed as the friend of every Christian and benevolent work. The day he died was a day of general mourning and lamentation. About two thousand persons attended his funeral; and there were few of the negroes down whose cheeks, tears of bitter sorrow did not stream. The greatest order and solemnity prevailed whilst the military followed the corpse to the grave, and the missionary Nyländer read the funeral service of the Church of England.

Amongst the missionaries who fell victims to the fever were James Bunyer, schoolmaster at Freetown, who arrived in the colony on the 9th of January, and died in the following April; the Rev. W. H. Schemel, who went out in the same ship with Bunyer, and was laid in the grave beside him; and—saddest death of all—the Rev. W. Johnson, the faithful and successful pastor of Regent's Town.

Mr. Johnson's wife had returned to England in very feeble health; and on her arrival, she wrote to say that there was little or no hope of her recovery. Poor Johnson was, naturally, anxious to see her once more before her removal from this world, and having also some business of a domestic nature which required his presence for a time in Hanover, his native country, he sought and obtained permission from the Committee to pay a second visit to Europe. On the day after the death of Mr. Schemel, he went on board the "Betsy and Anne," apparently in the soundest health, and sailed for England. Three days after, the fatal fever developed itself. He had, doubtless, inhaled the deadly poison before his departure from Africa. Four days he hovered between life and death, and then his spirit went "unto God who gave it;" not, however, before he had expressed his unwearying confidence in Christ his Saviour, his gratitude to God who had enabled him to sow the good seed of eternal life in Africa, and his undoubted conviction that he was about to receive the crown of righteousness which the Lord, the righteous Judge, would give him.

"Truly Johnson was a burning and a shining light; and the Christian might well be pleased to exchange for his seven years of eminent usefulness and 'life in earnest'—he was but thirty-seven when he died—the longer span of ineffectual life often wasted here below. His example is specially seasonable. It shows us how many hidden gems there are that the world knows nothing of, which are to glitter at the last day in the Redeemer's diadem; it shows us what is the missionary message which

God authenticates and owns; and it shows us the style of man needed as an evangelist to the heathen. Preach free grace and preach it fully, heartily, prayerfully, and you will not preach in vain. We need such men for missionaries now. Feeble, irresolute, half-hearted men, with little experimental knowledge of their own hearts, and Christ's love— these are not the 'good soldiers of Jesus Christ.' It is in this view that we ask our friends to add William Johnson's outline to their gallery of missionary portraits when they wish to know the sort of men suitable for such a work."*

Of the character and labours of Mr. Johnson Sir Charles McCarthy wrote:—"It is a severe dispensation öf Providence upon us. His exertions have been very great, and may, perhaps, be equalled, but will never be surpassed. He was esteemed by the whole community. His people feel as they ought, having lost in him a father and a friend."

Two other clergymen, not missionaries, but zealous and earnest men, who took a deep interest in the spiritual welfare of the Africans, were also removed by the yellow fever at this time.

The Rev. Samuel Flood, colonial chaplain, having obtained a short leave of absence, embarked with his wife for England, a few days after Mr. Johnson sailed; and he, too, died on board ship shortly after his departure from Africa.

* Church Missionary Intelligencer, Nov., 1852.

The Rev. Henry Palmer, assistant colonial chaplain, took Mr. Flood's place during his absence; and although gifted with a strong constitution, and accustomed to the temperature of Western Africa, by a long residence in warm climates, the dreadful fever, which was desolating the coast, laid him low.

Mr. Palmer had, in early life, served in the army, and writing of his death, the missionary Nyländer said:—"There cannot be a more honourable death than that of the late Mr. Palmer. Had he died in the battle of Waterloo, when he fought there, he would have died as a brave soldier, in the service of his king and country, and his death would have been counted honourable; but here he died in the battle which he had begun to fight in the service of the King of kings and Lord of lords; and nothing less than a crown of eternal glory, which fadeth not away, is his reward."

The dark catalogue of deaths is not yet full. The Rev. C. W. Beckaner, who arrived in the colony in January, 1823, died of the fever in the following June. Mr. and Mrs. Düring escaped the fever, but only to die another equally terrible death. They embarked in the "Hadlow," for England, on the last day of August, and in the beginning of November the ship went down, with all on board, in one of those fearful gales so common in the English Channel. They had confronted without dismay the withering blast of African pestilence;

and there is reason to believe that they did not lose their faith in God when exposed to the terrors of the raging sea. They had learned calmly to look death in the face, and now, when their work was done, and their conflict over, the Heavenly Pilot brought them to the haven where they earnestly desired to be.

The deplorable circumstances of the year 1823 led the Committee of the Church Missionary Society seriously to consider the best means of supplying the vacancies which existed in the ranks of the missionary band, and also the best way to provide for the requisite number of teachers as the demand for them arose.

It was resolved to propose to the Government that the Committee should undertake to pay the stipends of all the English clergymen who were required for service in the colony; these clergymen to be approved by the King through the Secretary of State for the Colonies; also that the Committee should maintain the schools at Freetown, and the Christian Institution at Regent's Town. The Government, on the other hand, should be required to provide, in each of the country parishes, for the education of the inhabitants under the authority and direction of the parish clergyman, besides erecting churches and schools with houses for the clergy and schoolmasters, and granting a sufficient amount of land with each house.

A deputation consisting of the Bishop of Litchfield, Lord Calthorpe, Lord Bexley, Mr. Parry, and others, laid this proposal before Earl Bathurst. After some slight modifications it was agreed to on the part of the Government, and entered amongst the rules of the Church Missionary Society.

This was the commencement of another important period in the history of missionary enterprise at Sierra Leone.

The year 1824 was marked by a signal calamity—the death of Governor Sir Charles McCarthy, who fell in an engagement with a party of Ashantees at Cape Coast Castle. The Ashantees are noted for their ferocity and for their treachery.* Human life they regard as of little or no value. When Richard and John Lander, the African travellers, complained on one occasion to an Ashantee chief that some of his subjects annoyed them by intruding into their tents, the chief replied:—"Take your guns and shoot a few of them. You have full permission from me to do so. When you have shot five or six, the rest will not venture to molest you." It is said that after Sir C. McCarthy fell in the skirmish with the Ashantees, the chiefs ate his heart that they might become equal to him in valour, and his dried flesh and bones were divided amongst the people as charms to inspire courage.

It is due to the memory of Sir C. McCarthy to

* Whilst I write these lines our brave countrymen in West Africa are again engaged in deadly conflict with the Ashantees.

record here that he was all through the period of his administration the friend and benefactor of the African race, as well as an earnest supporter of the projects of the Church Missionary Society. The Chief Justice of Sierra Leone, in the address which he delivered shortly after the death of Sir Charles, at Quarter Sessions, said :—" Look at the state of the colony when he arrived, and look at it now. Look at the difference in Freetown, in the inhabitants, in the resources, in the importance of the colony; but above all look at the liberated Africans and their villages. Could the gentlemen present who have themselves seen it, have otherwise believed the change that has taken place? To say nothing of the churches, the houses, the cultivated fields which are everywhere occupying what was previously a dark impenetrable forest, look at the change in MAN. Is the man who worships his God as a Christian, who daily performs all the duties of civilized and social life as a duty for which he knows himself to be answerable—and many of whom are now in this room as constables and jurymen—are these the degraded ignorant beings scarcely equal to the brute, whom British philanthropy rescued from destruction, from the hold of the slave ship, from slavery both of body and mind? The change has been miraculous. The finger of God is here. But our late lamented Governor was the instrument of Almighty mercy to these poor creatures. And well and faithfully, through every difficulty, through every danger did he perform his duty to its utmost extent. He has laid the foundation, he has commenced the superstructure of African civilization, of the improvement of the negro race, of the extension of Christianity over this vast continent so firmly that even his loss, great as it is, cannot long retard it."

Another event—one of a pleasing and cheering character—marked this year 1824. It was the laying of the foundation stone of St. John's church, at Charlotte. Where a few years before no sound had been heard except the fierce leopard's howl or the hoarse bark of the prowling wolf, several hundreds of Europeans and Africans were assembled together to lift up voices of prayer and praise to God, and to invoke His blessing on the sacred edifice which they were about to erect to His honour and glory.

The next three years were years of heavy trial. One earnest Christian labourer after another was cut down. Amongst others, Nyländer, for twenty years a faithful missionary, was numbered with the dead. The gaps that were made in the ranks of "the noble army of martyrs" were so great that congregations were frequently left without the instruction and superintendence to which they had become accustomed, and a process of moral deterioration soon commenced, which it appeared almost impossible to arrest. At Regent and Gloucester especially, where the success of the Society's missionaries had, at first, been so great, the declension in spiritual religion was most manifest. "Regent," wrote the Rev. Henry Brooks, "is certainly a different place from what I had conceived it to be. I found all mouths open against it, many things in sad disorder, but nothing to cast me down. That a great work has been done here, no one can deny: but whether to the extent which most imagine I very much doubt."

Mr. Brooks found the Christian Institution which had been established at Regent for the training of native teachers in the greatest confusion; the buildings deserted, and the pupils scattered in all directions; but re-commencing operations with three youths, he endeavoured to restore the institution to its original purpose, and in a great measure he succeeded. This was in February, 1825. Three months after, he, like so many of his predecessors, was struck down, and Mr. Davey, the schoolmaster of Leopold wrote:—"We are at this moment overwhelmed with sorrow. I have just returned from the funeral of our very dear brother, the Rev. Henry Brooks of Regent. We this day see Regent in a state in which it never was before, since the Rev. W. Johnson first took charge of it, without a single permanent European teacher, and who can be found to supply the vacancy I know not."

There were, at the beginning of 1825, fourteen stations in the colony under the Society's care, and at these stations were employed seven clergymen, seven schoolmasters, ten schoolmistresses, three native teachers, and seventeen native assistants—making a total of forty-four; which, however, before the end of the year was reduced by death and other causes to thirty-two—a number far below what was required to secure efficiency in the carrying on of missionary work. Under the circumstances the mission was very far from flourishing. In fact the language employed by the missionaries who remained at their posts was the language of despondency amounting almost to despair. In their letters to friends at home they dwelt on the hopes of the future, and not as they had been wont to do, on the successes of the past or the triumphs of the present. The West African Mission Report for 1825 speaks of the indifference towards the public means of grace manifested at some of the stations; of the smallness of the contributions to the Society's funds; and of the lamentable cases of some, who having made an open profession of religion, had not lived in a manner consistent with that profession.

The mission field, however, had not become wholly barren. It had only suffered by comparison with its previous fertility. Some verdant spots still remained to give promise of future renovation; and looking at these verdant spots, Mr. Ruban, who drew up the Report mentioned above, concluded his statement with these words:—" The mission to this colony is undoubtedly one which requires, in a peculiar manner, the exercise of faith; but when it is considered what the Lord has already done for His servants both here and in England in not suffering their hands to hang down, but enabling them steadfastly to maintain the post of duty, unwearied by toils and undismayed by dangers, it is not surely too much to hope that He will yet be with them in every future trial; and at length, when the time appointed in His unerring counsels shall have arrived, will abundantly prosper their labours."

A new and important feature now began to be developed in the Society's work—the formation and employment of a native agency. The severe losses which the mission had sustained by the death of many European missionaries had induced the committee to turn their attention to the raising up of a body of native pastors and catechists. They therefore resolved to lose no time in educating a number of intelligent and pious natives of Africa, who should in due time become christian teachers amongst their countrymen. With what energy and with what happy results this resolution was carried out, will be seen in the course of this narrative.

The Christian Institution already mentioned as having been established at Leicester, and afterwards removed to Regent's Town, was closed in 1826, and a new institution was established at Fourah Bay between Freetown and Kissey. At Michaelmas, 1826, there were six African youths in the institution who anxiously desired to be trained as native ministers. Their names were Samuel Crowther, John Harvey, James Jones, John Pope, John Wright, and William Tamba. The reader hardly needs to be told that the first name on this list is the name of one whose services in the cause of African missions will be remembered as long as the world lasts—the present Bishop of the Niger. Two years after his admission to the Fourah Bay institution, Crowther was appointed native school-master at Regent, and thus began a career which has since been so successful and so distinguished.

I have thought it right to devote a whole chapter of this book to an account of the life and labours of this illustrious African Bishop.*

In the beginning of the year 1831, the effective force of the mission consisted of eight clergymen, five European catechists, and fourteen native school-masters. There were under the care of these, nine congregations and fifteen schools containing 2360 pupils. During the previous five years, sickness had attacked many; death had removed some; and, worse still, the Rev. Thomas Davey, one who had been amongst the most valued of the Society's

* See Chapter VIII.

ordained missionaries was proved to have been guilty of gross misconduct. Referring to this, the Rev. C. L. F. Haensel said in a letter to the Committee:—" The difficulties in which this melancholy affair involves us are great. For the present I will only say that your missionaries will endeavour to bear up under the pressure ; but we cannot hide it from ourselves that the mission has been shaken to its base."

The number of communicants in all the stations in 1831 was 683. The candidates for admission to the Holy Communion were 294; the baptisms were 77 ; the pupils in the day schools amounted to 1338 ; those attending the Sunday schools to 684 ; and those in the institution, including students and probationers, to 12.

Mr. Haensel, however, who was at the head of the institution, never ceased to regret that his duties as a missionary interfered greatly with the duty which he owed to his pupils. So much of his time was occupied outside the institution that it was impossible for him to enter minutely into the feelings and views of those who had been placed under his instruction. The consequence was, that occasionally there was much to deplore in the conduct of the pupils.

The same lack of vigilance was felt at all the stations, the consequence was the discovery of open scandals even amongst the communicants and candidates for baptism. Excommunication was resorted to in several cases, and a slight check was thus placed on those who were inclined to be disorderly.

Much as there was at this time to be regretted, there was still a great deal to encourage; and the Committee of the Church Missionary Society did not hesitate to push on heartily towards the goal which they aimed at reaching. In their 33rd Annual Report, they thus express themselves:—
"The work of this Society has been one of continued and loud appeal to the mercifulness of Christians in this nation; nor has the voice of pity ever been silenced, notwithstanding the great sacrifice of valuable lives which has been incurred in the progress of our labours. The Committee feel, moreover, that they are justified in using the strong term *progress* when speaking of the character of the Society's exertions in Sierra Leone. In a population of 21,000 liberated Africans, of whom about 12,000 come more particularly under the charge of our missionaries, they can point out this result—that about 3000 are constant attendants on public worship; 3000 children and adults are under education, and there are 694 communicants under Christian discipline. It is not a time, therefore, to be disheartened, but to persevere; under the sure persuasion that the Church of Christ, once firmly planted on this Western coast, shall break forth northward,

and southward, and eastward, till all the tribes of Africa acknowledge Him as Lord who is 'above all, through all, and in us all.'" "

The death of the Rev. John Godfrey Wilhelm, in 1834, removed from the mission field the last surviving representative of the first efforts made by the Society to introduce the gospel amongst the native tribes beyond the colony. He arrived in Africa in December, 1811; and for more than twenty-three years he was never absent from his work, having all that time, without intermission, literally borne the burden and heat of an African day. During that period he had seen nearly one hundred of his fellow-labourers disabled or laid low; it had devolved on him to commit to their kindred earth many with whom he had entered into terms of Christian friendship and fellowship. He had outlived all the familiar faces of his early career as a missionary; and thus although he had not "attained unto the days of the years of the life of his fathers," being only fifty-six at the time of his death, he had nevertheless paid all the penalties of a lengthened old age in the desolation arising from the loss of friends. Mr. Kissling, writing at a time when the mission was in great trouble, thus bears his testimony to the character of his departed friend and fellow-labourer:—"While we were thus tryingly exercised, our very dear, aged, and venerable brother, the Rev. J. G. Wilhelm, was visited with affliction, that after suffering awhile he might be fully prepared to receive the divine summons to quit this vale of tears, of sin, and of sorrow, to enter into his heavenly rest and receive a crown of glory with "Well done! good and faithful servant!"

In the midst of these calamities there was one proof given of the improvement that was taking place in the people under the care of the missionaries, which, considering the previous habits of the Africans, is by no means unimportant. Matrimonial unions were becoming more frequent. In the river district, Mr. Kissling reported that seventy-two couples were united in holy wedlock within three months, some of whom had been living in an unlawful state for several years, without being in the least sensible that they were doing any wrong.

Regent, too, was beginning to raise its head. Thirteen persons, five men and eight women, were baptized, and of these John Attana, the native catechist, said:—"They had been well tried, so far as human power and knowledge could try them; and I can speak favourably concerning them that they have, so far as we have observed, conducted themselves agreeably to their profession, and have behaved themselves well, being very regular in the use of the means of grace, constantly attending the house of God, and other means appointed for their improvement."

In the next chapter some account will be given of

the Rev. Henry Townsend, the eminent missionary whose name is associated with the triumph of the gospel in Abbeokuta. In this place I will content myself with quoting his first impressions of a Sunday at Sierra Leone. He says:—" No one arriving here would imagine that he was in a country the inhabitants of which have been accustomed to idolatry, but in one where God had been many years worshipped in spirit and in truth. The solemn stillness of the day of rest reigns around; business and work are laid aside; and numbers of both sexes are seen hastening to school to learn to read and be instructed in the Christian religion. All are clean and as well dressed as their circumstances will allow. * * * * * *
During divine service they were attentive and devout, each one performing his or her part in the public worship of the day. This is the first Lord's Day which I have passed in Sierra Leone; and if every one be kept by the people as this has been, it shows that they honour God's laws, and that the Spirit of God has been with them, teaching and guiding them in the path of holiness to the praise and glory of that grace which has called them from darkness to light."

The mission received no accession of strength during the greater part of the year 1837.

In the early part of that year it was considered advisable for two of the catechists, Mr. Collins and

Mr. Croley, both of whom had suffered severely from illness, to try the effect of change of air, and accordingly they set out on a visit to the Banana and Plantain islands. These islands are made interesting by the reference to them in the Journal of the Rev. John Newton. It was on the Plantain Island that Newton was kept for fifteen months in captivity, an object of commiseration to the meanest slave. He says in his "Narrative:"— "Had you seen me, Sir, then go so pensive and solitary in the dead of night to wash my one shirt upon the rocks, and afterwards put it on wet that it might dry on my back while I slept; had you seen me so poor a figure that when a ship's boat came to the island, shame often constrained me to hide myself in the woods from the sight of strangers; especially had you known that my conduct, principles, and heart were still darker than my outward condition, how little would you have imagined that one who so fully answered to the 'hateful and hating one another' of the apostle, was reserved to be so peculiar an instance of the providential care and exuberant goodness of God." *

At the Kittam river, which is about a hundred and fifty miles from the Plantains, and which is particularly referred to in Mr. Newton's narrative, as being the place at which he was finally liberated from his captivity, the old people well remember

* Authentic Narrative by the Rev. John Newton.

the circumstance of the ship's calling in and carrying Mr. Newton away.

Just before leaving the islands in 1745, Mr. Newton planted some lime trees, which ninety years afterwards were green and flourishing. The Rev. W. B. Johnson mentions in his Journal a visit to these trees in 1820. They had been cut down, but from the trunk of one of them new branches had shot forth. On the solitary spot on which these lime trees grew, Newton passed many a day beguiling his hours with the study of Euclid, the only book in his possession. At that time and for years after he was of all men the most miserable, utterly reckless, a very outcast from society, wicked beyond all expression, despised by the meanest slave in Africa; yet he lived to become an eminent preacher of the gospel of Christ, to have his memory embalmed in the hearts of millions by his writings, and to take a prominent part in the founding of the Church Missionary Society, which has conferred such great and lasting benefits on Africa.

In the year 1839, the missionaries were particularly embarrassed by the vast additions which had been made to the population of the colony by the arrival of liberated slaves. During the preceding three years, not fewer than 13,000 recaptured slaves had been registered at Sierra Leone, and this number did not include the thousands who had been emancipated and registered in the West Indies, and who were, from time to time, transferred to Africa. Such an increase of the population had, as might have been expected, a retrograde influence on the state of civilization and on the spread of religion in the colony.

Greater exertion, therefore, was made by those to whom the work of the mission was entrusted; and the Rev. J. U. Graf feeling the utter impossibility of meeting by European aid alone the demand made for Christian labourers, adopted the plan of appointing native district visitors to act as assistants to the ordained missionaries. The plan adopted proved to be successful, and made it clear to all who were not blinded by prejudice, that native Christians possessed the ability to be useful to their countrymen, and that they might be placed, without danger, in the responsible position of witnesses for the truth of God in the midst of heathenish superstition. This was one of the first steps taken towards the appointment of native pastors, and the organization of a native church in Sierra Leone.

The schools throughout the colony were at this time in a most flourishing condition. To them especially, the good men who laboured for the advancement of true religion, looked as the greatest of all aids towards the ultimate destruction of heathenism. "We look," said Mr. Kissling "to the children of the liberated Africans with much interest and concern. They form the rising generation in Sierra Leone. It is therefore of the utmost importance to acquaint them early with the blessed truths of the gospel, and to instil into their minds the principles of civilization. They are also more capable of receiving instruction, as they understand and speak the English language much better than their parents. In the year 1836 the number of such children, with a few liberated Africans under our daily instruction, was 1765; in the year 1837 they amounted to 2034. Two new schools have since been opened—one at Waterloo, and the other at Kent; and there are now in 1838, no fewer than 2530 children attending our day schools."

Nor were Sunday schools neglected: "I wish," continued Mr. Kissling "our friends at home could have a sight of these schools. I am sure it would interest them to see apprentices, both male and female, and husbands and wives of thirty, forty, and fifty years of age, form a circle round their little teacher, perhaps not more than ten or twelve years old, learning the alphabet, steps to reading, and Scripture catechism."

The year 1840 was marked by many changes in the mission staff. Thirteen new missionaries arrived in the colony in the month of January, and before the end of July five of them had been cut off by the country fever, whilst five more had to return home in feeble health. But those who remained worked on courageously. It was, however, becoming every year more and more evident that without native aid European missionaries could hope to effect but little. Every effort, therefore, was made to develop the Fourah Bay Institution, and to make of it a nursery for the ministry of the African Church. It was resolved that it should be conducted on such a system as was best calculated to impart a sound education to the youths received into it, and thus become, under the divine blessing, the means of preparing Africans to be themselves the teachers of their own countrymen.

The work of the mission now promised to become permanent. Twenty-four years of unremitting toil had begun to tell on the spiritual and moral condition of the people. The gospel of Christ had indeed proved to be "the power of God unto salvation to every one that believed." In a country in which at the beginning of the century not a single Christian was to be found, there were at the close of the year 1840 to be numbered 6654 regular attendants on public worship, of whom 1362 were communicants. The number of schools was 51, in which sound instruction was given both in secular and religious subjects to 6026 pupils.

These results had not been obtained without the sacrifice of many valuable lives.

When the final assault was made upon Delhi during the Indian Mutiny of 1857, several brave men undertook the perilous task of blowing open the gate through which the British troops were to enter the city. They accomplished their task, but it was only at the sacrifice of the lives of several of the heroes forming this forlorn hope. Without their aid, however, the city could not have been taken. They, thinking only of the duty which fell to them, fearlessly advanced, shattered the gate which impeded the progress of their companions in arms, and a few hours afterwards India was saved, and British power was re-established from the Khyber Pass to Cape Comorin.

The action of the dauntless heroes of Delhi may serve to illustrate the conduct of the African missionaries of whom mention has been made in this chapter. They, too, led a forlorn hope, and removed obstacles which enabled their successors to gain possession of the spiritual citadel which they were assaulting. At the sacrifice of their lives they discharged their duty, and when that duty had been discharged they "died in faith not having received the promises, but having seen them afar off."

Writing of Christian missions in South India, the Rev. Dr. Norman Macleod says—and what he says applies with equal force to West Africa:—"Alas! how little is known and how little is remembered

of those noble men who alone and solitary, amidst lawless and fanatical heathen, held up the banner of the Cross, and were in God's sight the salt of the earth and the lights of the world.   *   *   *   *
Surely these heroes are as well worth being remembered and honoured by a Christian people as Lord Clive or Warren Hastings."

CHAPTER VI.

ONWARD STILL.

"Onward, therefore, pilgrim brothers,
    Onward with the Cross our aid ;
Bear its shame and fight its battle
    Till we rest beneath its shade !
Soon shall come the great awaking,
    Soon the rending of the tomb ;
Then the scattering of all shadows,
    And the end of toil and gloom."
                                    BARING GOULD.

DURING the year 1841 the British Government organized an expedition for the purpose of penetrating into the interior of Africa, and negotiating alliances with the native chiefs, which should have the effect of putting an end to the slave trade and substituting for it lawful commerce in the agricultural and other products of the country. This is known as the Niger Expedition. I shall have occasion in the course of this chapter to refer to the labours of the zealous men who carried out the object of the expedition; but a complete account of what they accomplished must be reserved until I have advanced a step further in my narrative of missionary work.

One of the great disadvantages under which

the mission laboured was that which arose from a constant change of those employed in the work. Many, as we have seen, were cut off by disease; others were compelled to return to Europe after a residence of a few years, sometimes of only a few months: and fresh levies were necessary to take the place of those whom death had cut down or whom the climate had disabled. In no portion of the mission field was this disadvantage felt more than in the Fourah Bay Institution, where that intimate knowledge of human character which long and familiar intercourse alone can give, was so much needed by the superintendent. The young men educated at the institution were designed for public and important offices; and the utmost caution, founded on the most careful judgment, was required in the selection of those to whom the duties of those offices were to be confided. It is quite clear that a clergyman who had held the office of Principal or Superintendent of such an institution for only a few months could hardly be expected to be sufficiently acquainted with the inmates to be able to form a correct judgment respecting them; and when we know how numerous were the changes that occurred in the staff at Fourah Bay, the wonder is, not that in some cases the native teachers throughout the colony disappointed the expectations formed of them, but that the mission was not materially injured by the misconduct and incompetency of some of them. This, however, was not the case, and in the midst of difficulties the work of Christian education went boldly forward.

On the 22nd of February, 1841, the foundation of a new church was laid at Gloucester, the ceremony being attended by the workmen and children. The building was completed on the 12th of August, and opened on the following day for divine service.

It is worthy of notice that the people for whose benefit the church was intended, contributed to its erection a large amount in free labour. They carried many hundreds of loads of sand and lime from Freetown, a distance of seven miles, over a mountain road, and on the day when the edifice was completed, between 600 and 700 persons assembled to join in the worship of Almighty God.

But not content with giving their labour, these African Christians gave liberally of such money as they possessed. In order to mark their appreciation of the efforts that had been made by their European brethren for their spiritual welfare, they voluntarily formed the Sierra Leone Church Missionary Association, and in the month of August, 1841, they remitted to England the sum of £87 16s. 5d. in token of their readiness to aid in extending to their countrymen the inestimable blessings which had been conferred upon them.

Each year contributions have been raised and forwarded for the same purpose; and each year like the ancient churches of Macedonia, "the abundance of their joy and their deep poverty have abounded unto the riches of their liberality."

Writing of the labours, difficulties, and progress which had characterized the mission up to the year 1841, Mr. Denton says:—"The question naturally arises, 'What are the results of your first years' labours in the new mission?' I confess that, to the casual observer and the enthusiast, little will appear; but to those who are experienced in the work of missions, and to us who are engaged in it, there is abundant cause for thankfulness, and encouragement to persevere. A second inquiry might be, 'What are the difficulties which you have had to encounter?' In reply to which, I think I may say they have been just such as might have been anticipated. Those which have arisen from the task of learning a new and barbarous language, have been by no means small; and others have resulted from the people not knowing or mistaking our real motive; but, perhaps, the greatest obstacle has been that total indifference to spiritual things which man, in his natural state, everywhere evinces. The Lord's Day has been proclaimed by the sound of a bell passing their doors. The people have been invited and entreated to attend, but after all only a few would assemble. This has led us to assume new ground—to go out into the highways and hedges, carrying the gospel into their streets and houses, and, as it were, compelling men to hear it. If these means can be carried out, I doubt not that much good will result; but here we feel our weakness, our numbers being so small, and our labours so often interrupted by sickness, that we can do but little in this way."

In the month of February, 1841, a new king was elected to succeed the sovereign from whom the missionaries had received the grant of land on which their settlement was erected, and who died the preceding year. The new ruler, or Ali Kali, as he was called in the native language, was crowned on the 13th of February, in the presence of the Governor of Sierra Leone and his family, attended by his staff and a military escort. The object of the Governor was to form a treaty with the new king and the surrounding chiefs.

"This treaty contains," says Mr. Denton, "some articles of considerable importance, such as, preventing the exportation of slaves, and allowing the residence of a British Consul, and the free ingress and egress of Europeans, with liberty to practise and teach the Christian religion. This, of course, is of peculiar interest to us; and occurring just as we are settling among them, we cannot but regard it as a favourable intimation from the Lord that we are, in this undertaking, under His guidance and protection, and may also confidently expect His blessing."

The Governor here referred to was Sir John Jeremie, who unfortunately died the following April.

It would appear as if the year 1842 were the turning point in the history of missionary enterprise at Sierra Leone. The reports of the officers engaged in the Niger Expedition had made it clear that if Africa was to be redeemed from misery, it must be by means of a native agency. Only Africans could carry out the Christian and philanthropic plans which alone could rescue the country from its wretched condition. And where were Africans fitted for such a work, to be obtained? God, in His providence, had turned the wickedness of man to the furtherance of His own gracious purposes of love. Dealers in slaves had brought from the interior large numbers of natives belonging to different tribes. These had been, as I have shown, liberated by the officers and crews of British ships, and conveyed to Sierra Leone, so that there existed in 1842, within the colony, the representatives of about forty different African tribes, who having received the gospel of Christ from the lips of European Christians, were willing to communicate it to their kindred and acquaintance in their respective homes.

A truly missionary spirit existed at that time amongst the Christians of Sierra Leone. At the anniversary meeting of the Church Missionary Association large numbers of Africans were present, some of them having travelled fourteen miles to take part in the proceedings.

The Annual Report which was adopted by that meeting referred to the great improvement which had taken place, and to the necessity that existed for native helpers. "The increase of numbers,"—these are the words of the Report—"the growing improvement among our people, and the thirst for knowledge, call for greater exertion, and more self-denying labour. But who is to carry on this work? The Society has long been convinced, by painful experience, that European constitutions are but ill adapted for enduring much fatigue in this climate, and that their ultimate hope of succeeding in the evangelization of this benighted continent, rests on the raising up and qualifying, through God's blessing, native schoolmasters, teachers, and ministers, whose constitutions are adapted to the climate, to carry forward that work which, through the grace of God, European zeal has, at an immense sacrifice, begun and sustained in this colony for nearly forty years."

The eyes of all who felt interested in the employment of native agency naturally rested on the Fourah Bay Institution; and earnest efforts were made to increase the number of students, to raise the standard of education, to appoint a clerical tutor, and to erect a much larger building for the accommodation of students. The chief design of the institution, from the beginning, had been the training of native youths as schoolmasters, and, if possible, as clergymen.

Here an interesting inquiry presents itself. What are the mental capabilities of the negro races? It has been the habit with many ill-informed persons to say that negroes are only one degree removed from the brutes in intelligence, and that no amount of labour expended on them would improve their condition. The past history of Sierra Leone gives a direct contradiction to this assertion. That history has shown clearly that negroes are just as capable of receiving instruction, and profiting by it, as Europeans are; and that when they have the same opportunity of mental culture afforded to them as Europeans have, they are equally capable of grasping difficult subjects. Amongst other proofs that this statement is true, I may refer to the course of studies pursued at the Fourah Bay Institution. Those studies are of a very advanced nature now; but even in 1842, when the institution was still in its infancy, and the African mind still immature, the pupils were examined, and answered most creditably in Bible history, in ecclesiastical and general history, in arithmetic, grammar, and geography. Those who can form any idea of the condition of the liberated negroes in 1816, will not fail to see in the fact above mentioned evidence of wonderful progress, and to appreciate the earnestness of the European workers, by whose untiring energy this great change had been brought about.

The great subject of anxiety at this time was the moral and spiritual enlightenment of the tribes whose representatives lived within the colony. The ardour of the Christian natives was intense. Meetings were held, proposals were discussed, funds were collected; every effort was made to arouse Christian sympathy, and a strong determination was expressed to preach the gospel to those who lived "in the regions beyond."

In consequence of the excitement which prevailed amongst the Yorubans, and their anxious desire to return to their native land, accompanied by a missionary, Mr. Henry Townsend was deputed to proceed to the Yoruba country to see whether anything of a permanent character could be done for the spiritual good of the emigrants from Sierra Leone and the natives; to ascertain the disposition of the kings of Badagry and of Abbeokuta towards missionaries; and to bring the children of chiefs and others to Sierra Leone for education.

On the 14th of November, 1842, Mr. Townsend started for the Yoruba country. His mission was regarded with immense interest by the natives, who not only expressed approval of the project, but contributed liberally towards the expenses that were necessarily incurred.

Mr. Townsend's visit led to the establishment of the Abbeokuta mission in 1845—a mission which has been singularly blessed by Almighty God, and which, after passing through fiery trials, has stood every test applied to it, and now presents the truth of God in all its purity in the midst of surrounding corruption.

The history of the Abbeokuta mission can hardly be said to be included in that of Sierra Leone. It was, rather, one of the results of the missionary work which, up to the time when Mr. Townsend went to the Yoruba country, had been carried on in the colony; and ever since that time, it has received all the sympathy and all the support which the residents in the colony could give. But although not forming, strictly speaking, a portion of the work which I have attempted to describe in this narrative, it may not be out of place to state a few facts, with a view to show what great and important results have followed Mr. Townsend's visit, undertaken, as we have seen, at the earnest request of the Yorubans who in 1842 happened to be residing in the colony.

Although Abbeokuta, the capital of the Yoruba country, could not be occupied by missionaries till 1846, on account of the death of a friendly chief named Sodeke, the pioneers of the good work were usefully employed in the interval at Badagry, where a mission has been maintained ever since.

When, however, missionaries did settle at Abbeokuta, they found that the work which they had undertaken was singularly difficult, and that the risks by which they were surrounded were more than usually great. In 1851, the very existence of the mission was endangered by the invasion of the King of Dahomey, who, however, was happily repelled; and during the next few years there was marked progress and expansion, fresh centres of work having been taken up in several important places, one of which, Ibadan, ranks with Abbeokuta, not only as regards population, but as regards influence and power. Unfortunately, the recurrence of wars between rival tribes, or between sub-divisions of the great Yoruba tribe, has led to disastrous consequences. In 1862, the town of Ijaye, occupied by the Church Missionary Society in 1853, was utterly destroyed by the Ibadans, and out of a population of 40,000, those who escaped famine, and sword, and death by torture, were cruelly driven out of their own territory, and scattered all over the land. Shortly afterwards, another town, Awaye, an out-station of the Church Missionary Society, shared the same fate.

Another result of these wars was, that the communication between Ibadan and the coast was cut off, and the European missionaries in Ibadan were reduced to the greatest misery for want of the necessaries of life. In 1863, the King of Dahomey again threatened Abbeokuta, destroying on his march Ishagga, another of the towns occupied by the Church Missionary Society as a station. One-third of the population was killed on the spot, and the rest carried into captivity. Of those who were carried away, several were afterwards beheaded at Abomey, the capital of the kingdom of Dahomey.

Although in 1863 the invading host of Dahomey did not advance beyond Ibara, the year after Abbeokuta itself was attacked. After a bloody battle, the Dahomians were driven back, routed with great slaughter, and pursued into their own territory by the victorious Egbas. The difficulties of the Dahomians, both during their advance, and during their retreat, were increased by their own cruelty; for their previous raid had converted the country between their own frontier and Abbeokuta into a wilderness, and they found it hard to obtain the means of subsistence.

The mission at Abbeokuta was thus preserved, by God's good providence, from the perils which threatened its very existence. But another trial of a most serious character befel the European missionaries. In the month of October, 1867, a disorderly mob, taking advantage of the ill-will and jealousy which had long been felt by some of the native chiefs and elders, plundered and destroyed the mission premises, and the European missionaries were compelled shortly after to leave the city.

Two years later Mr. and Mrs. Hinderer, who had resided at Ibadan ever since 1852, were obliged, by failure of health, to return to England; and as the road from the coast to Ibadan has remained closed to the present moment, the native church there as well as at Abbeokuta has been left to its own resources. Notwithstanding these untoward circumstances, the work commenced by Europeans has in both places continued to grow and prosper, and the native Christians have learned in a greater degree than could have been expected, to rely less on human help and more on Christ, the great Head of the Church.

To return to Sierra Leone. The feeling which had influenced the Yorubans manifested itself also amongst the people called Nufi. The number of Nufis in the colony was small. Mr. Schön estimates the number of the whole nation at about 100,000, and says that their language is spoken from the confluence of the Tshadda with the Niger, along the left bank of the Niger to beyond Rabba. A copy of "Schön and Crowther's Journal" having fallen into the hands of some of them, they read with great interest that part of it which related to the manners and customs of their own people: and a hint was thrown out that it might be possible to send thither a missionary of their own nation. Home with all its associations presented itself to their minds; meetings were held for consultation, and a plan was formed which was communicated by delegates appointed for the purpose, to the missionary Committee in the colony. This was to send to the Nufi nation Joseph Bartholomew, a native schoolmaster, in order that he might instruct the people in the truths of the gospel. The request was accompanied with a contribution of £10 towards defraying expenses. It does not, however, appear that the request of the Nufi delegates was ever attended to by the Committee.

In 1843 the mission sustained a heavy loss in the deaths of Mr. W. C. Thompson and his wife. Mr. Thompson had been employed as a linguist and translator. In 1841 some merchants and other persons resident at Freetown, being anxious to extend the intercourse between Sierra Leone and the Foulah country for the purposes of commerce, Mr. Thompson was requested to proceed to Teembo, which lies about 400 miles north-east of the colony. This he consented to do, hoping to have opportunities for promoting the moral and spiritual welfare of the people, whilst he endeavoured to establish commercial relations with them. He was cordially received wherever he went, and although the Foulahs are strict Mohammedans, he was promised every assistance towards the establishment of Christian schools. For eleven months he heroically braved the greatest perils and underwent terrible privations. But when he had nearly succeeded in obtaining from the sanguinary Foulah chief, Omar, a promise that he would receive and protect Christian missionaries, he was removed from his earthly toils and sufferings after four days' illness, at Darah, near Teembo, on the 26th of November, 1843. Mrs. Thompson had died a few weeks before in Sierra Leone.

One of the encouraging circumstances of this year was the completion of a new church at Waterloo. It was a substantial stone building, capable of containing upwards of 600 adult persons, and between 200 and 300 children, who occupied a gallery by themselves. It was the sixth church erected at the expense of the Church Missionary Society. Mr. Warburton, writing on August 9th, 1843, says:—"I preached in Waterloo church. Though a week day, the place was filled. It is with grateful feelings to Him who giveth the increase, that I observe how abundantly it has pleased God to bless the labours of His servants at this village. Not quite six years ago, missionary work was recommenced at this station; and now there is a flourishing day school of 377 children; a Sunday school of 257 adults; a large congregation regularly hearing the word; 70 candidates for baptism; 51 communicants; and to crown the whole, a substantial church has been built under the superintendence of Mr. Young, capable of containing 900 persons."

Less than two years after—in February, 1845—the new buildings at Fourah Bay were commenced, the old house having become very much dilapidated. For thirty years the mission had struggled amidst perils and disasters. It had now arrived at maturity; and the first indication of its strength was the activity with which it made preparations to carry the Gospel into heathen regions by means of well educated and properly qualified clergymen and catechists.

The first stone of the new institution was laid by His Excellency Lieutenant-Governor Ferguson, who, after the ceremony had concluded, addressed the assembly. In his address he stated this fact, and as he stated it he was hardly able to repress his feelings, that "on the very spot where they were preparing to erect a building, whence it was hoped that spiritual freedom would be imparted to many Africans, there stood, forty years ago a *Slave Factory.*"

On the subject of education, as I have already said, there was a growing intelligence among those members of the liberated African class, who by industry and good conduct had risen to independence. To meet the demand for education of a higher grade than the village schools supplied, the Grammar School for boys, and the Female Institution for girls were established. Respecting these schools the Governor of Sierra Leone thus wrote in

one of his despatches to the Home Government:—
"Boarding schools," he said, "for the education of children of both sexes, have been established under the auspices of the Church Missionary Society; and so far the scheme promises well. It will, at no remote date, be the means of establishing a new, most important, and influential grade in the society of Sierra Leone; among which the husbands, the wives, and the domestic intercourse of the middle classes of England will, for the first time, find representatives in Western Africa. It may be taken as neither an unfair nor unfavourable criterion of the position in the social scale at which the people have arrived, that these establishments are at length acknowledged to have become necessary, and that the pecuniary means of many of the more industrious and successful of the people are now such as to enable them to avail themselves of the advantages which they afford.

"There has been an increase in the total number of children educated in the schools of the colony of 1528 scholars over the numbers of last year. The cause of education has assuredly borne its full share in the generally progressive advancement of the colony.

"The progress has not, however, been confined to mere numerical increase. Along with that, measures have also been adopted for affording to the children of the colony that which the progressive prosperity of its people has now made a desideratum, viz., an educational course of a higher character than that which merely qualifies for the labourer and the tradesman, wherein the principles of either total or partial charity is to be abandoned."

Many of the Africans who had attended the mission schools showed a taste for the study of natural philosophy; and in order to develop that taste, lectures were occasionally given on scientific subjects, illustrated with such apparatus as could be obtained in the colony.

Thus, in addition to religious instruction there was given secular instruction which was calculated to promote the worldly advancement and the intellectual culture of those to whom it was imparted; and the mission proved a blessing even to those who felt little or no interest in that gospel which the missionaries made it their principal object to declare.

At the time of which I am now writing, idolatry had almost if not altogether disappeared from within the limits of the colony; but it still lingered in some of its accustomed haunts. In the villages to the east and north-east of Sierra Leone, were still to be found tribes who were sunk in all the superstitions of heathenism. With these tribes only native ministers and catechists could deal effectually, and the time had not yet come for the employment of a native ministry on anything like a large scale.

The slave trade too was still stealthily carried on. Wherever the vigilance of British cruisers could be evaded, there the infamous slave dealer landed and swept hundreds down to the coast to be transported across the broad Atlantic. Sometimes these wretched captives had the good fortune to meet on mid-ocean with some friendly English ship, and after a desperate struggle, of which they were compelled to be passive spectators, they found themselves once more free and under the protection of Britain's flag; but often, too often, their captors succeeded in slipping away unperceived, to reap the fruits of their unholy traffic in America.

Amidst all that was lovely at Sierra Leone, painful sights occasionally obtruded themselves, which reminded lookers-on of the very worst days of the slave trade.

"In going," writes the Rev. C. T. Frey, in 1845, "from Kissey to Freetown, I met with a scene of misery which made such an impression on my mind that I can scarcely forget it. About 400 emancipated Africans, old and young, of both sexes, were proceeding towards Kissey hospital. They had just come from the slave vessel and were in a most heart-rending condition. Some, not being able to walk, were carried, while others supported themselves by sticks, looking from the starvation they had endured on board more like human skeletons than living beings. I have since been informed that within a short time about a hundred of them died. What had these poor creatures done that they should be thus treated? It was the love of money, truly called the root of all evil, in those who are called civilized people, which had brought them into this condition. How much longer shall this outrage be committed? If Christians in Europe could have but one peep into such misery, they would fervently pray for the propagation of the gospel of peace in Africa, and more actively engage in abolishing the slave trade."

Besides the existence of idolatry, and the occasional irruptions of the slave traders, there was yet another drawback to the satisfaction which the faithful missionary might feel in view of what had been accomplished in and around Sierra Leone. Petty wars raged with hardly any intermission between the various tribes whose possessions skirted the colony. These wars were generally attended with circumstances of great cruelty. The victors, in most cases, inflicted the severest punishment they could devise on the conquered; and when those who had once been conquered and punished became in their turn, by the chances of war, victors, they seldom failed to retaliate with tenfold cruelty the injuries which they had formerly suffered themselves.

To all these circumstances, calculated to depress the spirit of the most sanguine labourer in the mission field, we may add the continued mortality amongst Europeans of all classes. Deaths indeed were so frequent that the missionary work always possessed more or less the character of a "forlorn hope." In the course of the first twenty years, no fewer than fifty-three missionaries or missionaries' wives died at their post; being nearly an average of three every year. In the year 1823 out of five who went out, four died within six months. Two years after, six more went out. Two fell within four months of their landing in Africa. The next year three more went out; two of these died within six months.

These facts were, of course, well known at home, and yet the Church Missionary Society has never lacked a constant supply of willing labourers. This furnishes a sufficient answer, if any were needed, to those who deny the existence of Christian heroism amongst Protestant missionaries, and who reserve all their admiration for Romish monks, and for the followers of Ignatius Loyola and Francis Xavier.

Amongst those who in the year 1845 were laid in the "white man's grave," was Mrs. Gollmer, wife of the Rev. C. A. Gollmer, one of the pioneers of the Abbeokuta mission. She was buried at Badagry, and as she was the first person who had ever received Christian burial in that place, the scene was one never to be forgotten by those who witnessed it. Many of the natives out of curiosity accompanied the funeral party to the churchyard, and there learned the difference between the devilish rites which are observed at the burial of a heathen, and the solemn committal to the earth of the body of a Christian "in sure and certain hope of the resurrection to eternal life."

"The scene of this day," writes the Rev. S. Crowther, now Bishop Crowther, "will not soon wear away from the minds of those who were present, about 150 persons. The chiefs having been informed of our mournful bereavement, sent their messengers to express their sympathy with us: although not worshippers of the great God who made all things, yet they invariably ascribed this afflictive visitation to the providence of God, who knew and ordered all the events of life in His secret wisdom. Truly, although they know Him as God, 'they glorify Him not as God, but become vain in their imaginations, and their foolish heart is darkened.'"

And yet another sad death we have to record here, that of Mrs. Bultmann, the wife of the Rev. F. Bultmann. She had made it her especial duty, ever since her arrival in the colony, to try and improve the character and the condition of the native women. To the widows and children she proved herself a kind friend; and by all the members of her husband's flock she was looked up to with respect and affection.

Mr. Warburton says of her:—"She was a true Christian, and an excellent missionary's wife. Her kind, gentle, and unobtrusive manners were obvious to all; and those who have had the opportunity of spending any time under the hospitable roof of our dear brother, must feel that he has lost a helpmate not only in domestic affairs, but also in his missionary labours. Mrs. Bultmann was diligent in improving the female children in needlework, and in instructing them in religious and useful knowledge, but she did not confine her labours to them. I have seen adults also come to her statedly for instruction in the Word of God; and I have been surprised to hear how well she spoke English, (for German was her native language,) and to observe how scripturally she taught them."

Here let me say that, in the lives and deaths of such women as Mrs. Gollmer and Mrs. Bultmann, we have a sufficient answer to the assertion that Protestant missionaries are hampered in their work by their wives and children, and that only Romish ecclesiastics, who are forbidden to burden themselves with domestic cares, can properly discharge the duty of Christianizing the heathen.

I might, in all fairness, say to those Protestants who eulogize Romish missionaries, that the religion which is taught to the heathen by the priests of the Church of Rome differs very materially from that which was taught by the Lord Jesus Christ and

His apostles—that it is, in fact, a corruption of Christianity, a compound of Christianity and Paganism, in which the Paganism decidedly preponderates. I might, without difficulty, show that the celibacy of the clergy is nowhere recommended, still less commanded, in the New Testament; and that the first person who made it obligatory in the Roman communion, was Gregory VII, better known as Hildebrand the Great, who ascended the Papal throne in the eleventh century.

But I prefer to place my argument on lower ground, and to ask which of the two, the Protestant or the Romish missionary, exhibits to the heathen the loveliness of true religion, as seen in the domestic circle, and in the exercise of those affections which naturally spring up within a Christian household?

Look at the Romish priest sent forth at the bidding of the *Congregatio de Propagandâ Fide*, to West Africa, to combat heathenism. He goes as a lone man. He lives in solitude. He has no companion of his leisure hours. No sound of innocent mirth is ever heard within his dwelling; no boisterous laugh, the music of children's hearts, no pattering of merry little feet. He has no wife to whom he can confide his sorrows, or with whom he may share his joys. In sickness he has none to tend him. Strangers smooth his pillow, and administer the draught which is to cool his fevered lips. He stands aloof from all. In him all the sources of the purest and noblest affections are dried up. He can have no sympathy with his flock. Their teacher, so far as the scantiness of his knowledge permits him, he may be; their friend and counsellor he can hardly ever be. He lives in an atmosphere different from that in which those live by whom he is surrounded. All his affections are centred on Rome; all his desire is to obey the laws of the Sovereign Pontiff; all his anxiety to swell the numbers, by any means which circumstances may suggest, of those who belong to what he falsely deems to be the only church of Christ upon earth. He is a minister and peer of a stupendous empire which claims to extend over the whole globe. Like the envoy of some foreign government, he respects the authority of the chief in whose country he happens to live, but he regards the Pope as his lawful sovereign, and the furtherance of the Pope's designs as the object for which he was ordained and sent forth. Social progress for him can have no charms, except so far as it contributes to the advancement of Papal dominion; and of domestic happiness he can know little or nothing. He is a man with one fixed idea before him; and that, an idea which can hardly commend itself to the heathen people amongst whom he labours. In heathen as in Christian countries, abroad as at home, there can exist no real sympathy between a people under the influence of the domestic affections, and a cold, calculating, selfish, because celibate, clergy.

The Protestant missionary presents to the heathen in West Africa, as elsewhere, a picture the very reverse of this. He is a father, not in the conventional sense in which the sacred word is used by the Church of Rome, but a father in reality, with a father's affections. He is a husband, and knows what pure love means. He understands, because he has himself felt, the difficulties and the trials, as well as the joys and the pleasures, which those relationships of husband and father entail. His household generally is, and ought always to be, a model Christian household, forming a striking contrast to that of the Pagan. His flock feel and know that between him and them there must be real sympathy. The missionary's wife has her own special work to do by the side of her husband. Upon her devolves the care and the superintendence of the women and girls, who are sure to find in her, if she be what her position requires her to be, a true and constant friend. Let those who are tempted to sneer at the notion of missionaries being married, consider what an incalculable amount of good has been done by missionaries' wives, what a bright example most of them have set, and what heroines most of them have been amidst difficulties that might have appalled the stoutest hearts. There is work, arduous but glorious work, for Christian women to do amongst the heathen, and they will not do that work the less efficiently because they are virtuous wives and tender-hearted mothers. The heathen requires to be taught by living examples, what a halo the gospel of Christ sheds on all the relationships of life, and what it is that constitutes the happiness of a Christian household.

The faithful Protestant missionary can have no object in view but to make known Christ as the Head of the Church, and to show, by the example of himself and his family, how blessed are the influences of Christ's religion where it obtains full sway. And when the annals of missionary work are completed, on many a page will be found recorded the glorious deeds of those women who have lived and died for Christ, within sight of the idolater, bearing testimony to the irresistible power of the cross.

We have followed the course of events to the close of the year 1845. "Onward still" was the motto of those who then continued to carry on the glorious work. Suffering and death were seldom absent, and it would not have been strange if those who had devoted themselves to missionary labour, longed to return to the European homes which they had left behind. But it is a remarkable fact, and one which has been over and over again substantiated, that in West Africa the longing of the missionary has been to remain at his post, and to continue his work so long as life lasted. Often and often the declaration has been made by those who were cut off prematurely, and were about to be laid in an African grave, that they cheerfully surrendered their lives, and that they saw no reason to regret having undertaken the good work from which death was so soon to sever them. They did their duty nobly as "good soldiers of Jesus Christ," and when, in the discharge of their duty, they fell, they counted it all honour to die so glorious a death. This is emphatically the Lord's work, and it is marvellous in our eyes.

"The vessel," says the Rev. S. A. Walker, "that carries a missionary to Sierra Leone, bears no ordinary freight; and if Cæsar could think that his name and fortunes might set the angry elements at defiance, a greater conqueror than Cæsar may look calmly on nature in her angriest mood, whenever that ship breasts the Atlantic, which carries a messenger of the gospel to the pestilential shores of West Africa."

CHAPTER VII.

THE NIGER EXPEDITION.

"Good news! all ye that wander wide,
  Poor scattered sheep long torn and tried,
    In death and sin's domain :
The gracious Lord His Spirit sheds
O'er broken hearts and weary heads,
    To give them rest again.

Good news, idolaters! no more
Your altars black with fire and gore,
    Shall leave yourselves unclean ;
Th' atonement you can never find,
The blood that hallows all mankind
    Christ's Holy Cross hath seen."
                CHURCH MISSIONARY GLEANER.

I HAVE already said that the object of the Niger Expedition was to endeavour to put a stop to the slave trade by showing the native African chiefs the impolicy as well as the cruelty of continuing to carry it on ; and also to try and substitute for the slave trade, lawful commerce in the agricultural and other products of the country.

The view entertained by her Majesty's Government on this subject was explained in a letter addressed by Earl Russell—then Lord John Russell, and holding office as Colonial Secretary—to

the Lords of the Treasury, under date December 26th, 1839. In this letter Lord Russell says:—
"Her Majesty's confidential advisers are compelled to admit the conviction that it is indispensable to enter upon some new preventive system, calculated to arrest the foreign slave trade in its source by counteracting the principles by which it is now sustained. Although it may be impossible to check the cupidity of those who purchase slaves for exportation from Africa, it may yet be possible to force on those by whom they are sold, the persuasion that they are engaged in a traffic opposed to their own interests, when correctly understood.

"With this view, it is proposed to establish new commercial relations with those African chiefs or powers, within whose dominions the internal slave trade of Africa is carried on, and the external slave trade supplied with its victims. To this end the Queen has directed her ministers to negotiate conventions or agreements with those chiefs and powers, the basis of which conventions would be—1st, the abandonment and absolute prohibition of the slave trade: and 2ndly, the admission for consumption in this country on favourable terms, of goods, the produce or manufacture of the territories subject to them. Of those chiefs, the most considerable rule over the countries adjacent to the Niger and its great tributary streams. It is therefore proposed to despatch an expedition which would ascend that river by steam boats as far as the points at which it receives the confluence of some of the principal rivers falling into it from the eastward. At these or at any other stations which may be found more favourable for the promotion of a legitimate commerce, it is proposed to establish British factories; in the hope that the natives may be taught that there are methods of employing the population more profitable to those to whom they are subject, than that of converting them into slaves, and selling them for exportation to the slave traders."

The attention of the Committee of the Church Missionary Society was naturally drawn to this enlightened and benevolent attempt on the part of the British Government to benefit Africa; and they were encouraged to indulge the hope that the expedition might open the way for carrying on missionary operations in the interior of that continent through the medium of one of her noblest rivers. They therefore applied to Lord Russell for permission to send with the expedition two persons connected with the Church Missionary Society, in order to collect such information as might enable them to decide on the practicability and expediency of forming a mission on the banks of the Niger. This permission was readily granted; and the persons selected by the Committee were the Rev. James Frederick Schön, and Mr. Samuel Crowther.

Mr. Schön had been for ten years a zealous missionary in Sierra Leone. He had become intimately acquainted with the native character, and possessed some knowledge of the native languages. He possessed energy and judgment, and was in every respect qualified for the important duty assigned to him.

Mr. Crowther was an African, then about thirty-three years of age, a catechist in the service of the Church Missionary Society, now the Bishop of the Niger. His eventful career will be related in a subsequent chapter. These two joined the expedition on its arrival at Sierra Leone. Mr. Schön was placed on board the "Wilberforce," and Mr. Crowther on board the "Soudan."

The command of the expedition was entrusted to Captain H. Dundas Trotter, R.N., whose ship, the "Albert," was so named in honour of the late Prince Consort. Commander William Allen, R.N., who had accompanied Lander in his last voyage, and had constructed a chart of the Quorra river, was appointed to the "Wilberforce;" and Commander Bird Allen, R.N., to the "Soudan." Each vessel carried a sufficient number of officers, and a crew consisting partly of Europeans and partly of Africans. The commanders of the three ships above mentioned, together with Captain Cook—well known for his skill and humanity in rescuing the crew of the "Kent" East Indiaman, when on fire in the Bay of Biscay—were appointed her Majesty's Commissioners to make treaties with the native chiefs. The Rev. T. O. Müller accompanied the expedition as chaplain; and several gentlemen were appointed by the African Civilization Society to investigate the resources of that part of Africa which is watered by the Niger. Dr. Vogel was appointed botanist; Mr. Roscher and Dr. Stanger, geologists; Mr. Frazer, zoologist; Mr. John Ansell, gardener and seedsman; and Mr. John Duncan, who had been an enterprising traveller in Dahomey and Ashantee, was to give the other members of the expedition the benefit of his past experience, and such advice as he might consider necessary.

The "Soudan" left England on the 17th of April, 1841, and the "Albert" and "Wilberforce" on the 12th of May following. As these two last-mentioned vessels steamed out of Plymouth Sound, the crews of all the vessels lying at anchor, manned their rigging, and gave three cheers, such as only British sailors know how to give.

The "Albert" arrived first at Sierra Leone, on the 24th of June; the other two vessels a few days after.

On the 28th June a special service was held in St. George's Church, Freetown, when the Rev. D. F. Morgan preached an excellent sermon, taking for his text the words:—"Who hath despised the day of small things?" and on the afternoon of the same day a prayer meeting was held in the church and was well attended.

Mr. Schön says that there was no want of people who were willing and even anxious to leave Sierra Leone in order to accompany the expedition. Seamen, labourers, interpreters, and mechanics, offered their services in great numbers; and although many of them, no doubt, were influenced by interested motives, there were some amongst them who were desirous of furthering the philanthropic objects for which the expedition was undertaken.

On the 2nd of July the expedition left Sierra Leone, and after visiting the African settlements of Siberia and Greenwell, Cape Coast Castle and English Accra, arrived at the mouth of the river Nun on the 9th of August. After crossing the bar on the 13th, the ships were detained there for some days, whilst stores were being removed from a transport vessel. Up to this time seven deaths had occurred; four from casualties during the voyage, one from apoplexy, and two from fever of a low typhoid character. One of the two who died from fever was Mr. J. W. Bach, mathematical instrument maker. A few cases of illness occurred on board the "Wilberforce," but by the time the ships reached Ibo all were perfectly well, and singularly cheerful. During the voyage to the Nun, religious services had been regularly held on board the ships.

Captain Trotter issued an official order for public prayer in the different vessels under his command. Mr. Schön spent all his spare time in making translations into the Haussa language; and Mr. Crowther was similarly employed with the Yoruba dialects.

On the 26th of August, King Obi, the chief of the Ibo country, sent one of his sons on board the "Wilberforce" to welcome the strangers. He was a fine-looking young man of twenty. Both he and his attendants were present at prayers. On being told that one object which the expedition had in view was to make known the contents of the Bible—a copy of which was shown to him—he listened with evident incredulity: and when told that the slave trade was a very bad thing, and that white men wished to put an end to it, he replied that if white people gave up buying, black people would give up selling slaves. He also said that he had always believed that God intended that black people should be slaves to the whites.

The Ibos, it was found, were in their way a religious people. The word "Tshuku" (God,) was continually heard among them. Tshuku is supposed to do everything. When a few bananas fell out of the hands of one of the Ibos into the water, he consoled himself by saying—"God has done it." Their notions of the attributes of God were found to be wonderfully correct; and their manner of expressing their opinions concerning God very striking. "God made everything," they said constantly, "and everybody, both whites and blacks." Some of their parables were intended to be descriptive of the perfections of God. "God has two eyes and two ears," they said, "one in heaven, the other on earth"—a way of expressing their belief in the omniscience and omnipresence of God. On the death of a person whom they regarded as good, they said: "he will see God." On the death of a wicked person—"he will go into fire." Mr. Schön states it as his opinion that they could not have derived these ideas from Christians, for they had never had any intercourse with them.

On the following day, August 27th, King Obi himself visited the "Albert." The motives which led to the sending of the expedition were explained to him; and his answers and cautious inquiries showed clearly that he was quite capable of entering into the spirit of all that was said to him.

When this had been done, Captain Trotter ordered Mr. Schön to read to him a translation of an "Address to the Chiefs and people of Africa." He showed signs of impatience before the paper was concluded, and said: "I understand it all, and am willing to do all that is in my power. What good can it do to tell it to me so many times?" Mr. Schön adds:—"Perhaps the style of my translation was not sweet enough for his ears, and my tongue not sufficiently Ibonized."

Obi was then informed that all the requisite arrangements would be made by the following morning; and that he would receive presents after signing the treaty. He seemed anxious to get back to his own house, and offered to take Mr. Schön and some of the ship's company with him in his canoe, an offer which was readily accepted, as Mr. Schön was anxious to discover whether Ibo would be an eligible place for a missionary station. He found the country one vast swamp. It was the rainy season, but even during what might by comparison be called the dry season, Obi acknowledged that his country was low and very wet.

He received Mr. Schön very kindly in his palace, and showed him his hundred and ten wives. Before the palace stood an idol, holding a pistol in his left hand and a sword in his right. This was the god of war. Expressing in a hasty manner to his wives his surprise at many things which he had seen on board the "Albert," Obi took leave of Mr. Schön and went off to his superstitious ceremonies, in which he was assisted by some of his priests. The ceremonies consisted chiefly in the sacrifice of several sheep, which were afterwards distributed amongst the people and eaten. Mr. Schön returned on board at seven in the evening, leaving the interpreter on shore to witness the proclamation of the treaty into which Obi had agreed to enter with the Queen of England. He certainly fulfilled his engagement, for he told his people that he had given up the slave trade for ever, and he prohibited all his subjects from engaging in it any more, threatening all who should violate his contract with England, with severe punishment.

A very trifling circumstance however served to create grave suspicion in the minds of some of Obi's subjects. One of them happened to see in the cabin of one of the medical officers on board, a human skull. He rather hastily concluded that it had belonged to a black man who had been killed by the Europeans for the sake of his skull. The same man noticed as he went through the ships of the expedition, pictures of the Queen and Prince Consort, and likenesses of other distinguished persons. These he mistook for idols which were reserved as objects of adoration; and remarked, that whilst we spoke against their idols, we took care to decorate our vessels with our own, which were superior to theirs in elegance and finish. The interpreter, however, succeeded in persuading such of the natives as had formed these opinions that our likenesses were not idols, and that the skull had not been obtained in the manner in which they suspected it had been.

When King Obi returned on board the "Albert" to sign the treaty, he was told that it was the custom for Christians to call upon God for His blessing in all their undertakings, and he was requested to kneel down with the officers of the ship whilst the chaplain offered up a suitable prayer. He knelt in prayer for the first time in his life; and when he rose from his knees he appeared extremely alarmed and agitated. He trembled and shook violently, and the perspiration rolled down his cheeks. He was evidently in an agony of mind. He then called so loudly for his idol or charm, that all who were on deck could hear him, and turning to the interpreter, he said that he thought the prayer was intended to do him some harm. The idol was brought to him by his priest, who was on deck, and he was about to exhibit some of his superstitious ceremonies in the Commander's cabin, when the interpreter succeeded in appeasing him and convincing him that no harm was intended to his person or anyone belonging to him. Mr. Schön says that he has witnessed similar scenes in Sierra Leone. Liberated Africans attending divine service for the first time feel greatly alarmed. Their notions of worship are very different from those of Christians. The idolatrous rites of negroes are either intended to avert injuries from themselves or to inflict them upon others. Mr. Schön relates a story descriptive of the ideas of the Ibo people concerning God. They believe that there is a certain town in their country where Tshuku gives answers to questions addressed to him, after the manner of the ancient Grecian oracle at Delphi.

An answer of this kind to an interesting query is recorded by Mr. Schön. There was a man in this country possessed of great riches, and like many of his friends or equals unwilling to part with them. Troubled by the thought which interrupted him in all his enjoyment that he had to die, he resolved to consult Tshuku. He told Tshuku that he had "plenty money, plenty wives, plenty things to eat," and that he was very unwilling to leave all behind and enter into an unknown world. He therefore wished to know whether Tshuku could tell him anything that he might do to enable him to live for ever. Tshuku told him that there was but one thing required of him, and if he would do that he would be sure to live for ever. "Good news!" replied the rich man; "only tell me what it is, and I will do it." Tshuku told him that he should never allow himself to fall asleep. The rich man promised to do it; returned to his house, called his friends together and made a great feast. Eating and drinking, music, singing, and dancing, continued all night; and no sleep came to the rich man's eyes. Towards morning, however, he put a little rum into his tumbler, and sat down on a bench. His eyes began to close. His tumbler dropped from his hand. He jumped up and said, "Ah! I no been asleep; I no sleep no more, only tumbler fall from my hand: Tshuku no can believe me sleep." "Well," said his friends, "you had better go ask Tshuku again;" and he started a second time for Tshuku's place. When he arrived there Tshuku said, "Now, rich man, how do you do? Have you slept since you were here?" "No," replied the rich man. "What," said Tshuku, "did not the tumbler fall from your hands?" The rich man, "he no open mouth again." "See rich man," said Tshuku, "this makes God to be God, because He never sleeps, and you to be man, because you *must* sleep."

The whole expedition left Ibo on the afternoon of the 28th of August, and passing several small villages, arrived on the 2nd of September at Iddah.

Iddah is beautifully situated on the left bank of the Niger; the population being estimated at five or six thousand. The situation is better than that of Ibo, but far from healthy for Europeans. Here, as at Ibo, the king voluntarily entered into an agreement to suppress the slave trade, and to protect Christian teachers. On the 6th of September, the "Wilberforce" ran aground near Iddah, and was not got off till two days after. The swamp too, which extended all around, began to tell on the health of the crews, and several cases of fever occurred. One man on board the "Albert" died.

Early on the morning of the 9th, the ships left Iddah and proceeded up the river, and two days after reached a place called Adda Kuddu about five miles from the confluence of the Niger with the Tshadda.

The journals of Mr. Schön and Mr. Crowther record at this part of the voyage, several deaths from African fever, caused doubtless by the heat, which was registered at 87° late in the evening in the shade.

At the confluence a bargain was concluded between the King or Attah and the chiefs of the expedition. The accredited agents of the King made over to the Crown of England the land from Beaufort Island to Sterling Hill inclusive, an extent of about twenty-five miles, with the right of the river or the free navigation to it. It was proposed to establish a model farm on the spot, and also, if possible, a missionary settlement,

This important business having been brought to a satisfactory issue, arrangements were made for the "Wilberforce" to enter the Tshadda, whilst the "Albert" and "Soudan" were to proceed up the Niger. So numerous, however, were the cases of fever, that Captain Trotter resolved to send the "Soudan," with all the invalids on board, back to the coast, in the hope that the sea air would restore them to health. The other two ships were to proceed up the rivers.

No sooner had the "Soudan" left than fever broke out on board the "Wilberforce." "The increase in the number of invalids," says Mr. Schön, "determined the Commissioners to send the

"Wilberforce" also down to the coast; and the "Albert," though thinly manned, will proceed up the Niger. I cannot express, in words, my feelings of disappointment at these events; for if my anticipations prove correct, we shall soon be on our way back to the coast without accomplishing the object of our mission." And then comes a sad announcement—an announcement prophetic of failure, and calculated to depress the most sanguine.

"Sept. 20th. I am sorry to record that two of the Commissioners, Captain W. Allen and Captain Cook are ailing."

They were obliged to proceed in the "Wilberforce" to the mouth of the river without delay. "She has more the appearance," writes Mr. Schön, "of an hospital than that of a man-of-war. The quarter deck as well as the forecastle and the cabins of the gun-room are full of patients. The sight of them is enough to move a heart of stone. The active botanist, the ever-stirring mineralogist, the robust engineer, officers of every rank, and sailors who have long faced every danger, are brought low by the overpowering influence of an unhealthy climate; and the few persons who are able to be on their legs are barely sufficient to render the sick that assistance which they so much need."

The "Soudan," with forty-three invalids on board,

commenced her return voyage on the 19th of September, commanded by Lieutenant Fishbourne, Captain Bird Allen having joined the "Albert." She reached the mouth of the river on the 21st, losing on the way her surgeon and one of the sailors. On their arrival at the mouth of the river, all the sick, except two who were too ill to be moved, were taken on board the "Dolphin," and conveyed to Ascension Island, where most of them completely recovered.

The "Wilberforce" followed the "Soudan," but did not reach the sea till the 29th of September. On the 1st of October she anchored in the port of Clarence, Fernando Po, having lost three officers by the fever. A week after she sailed for Ascension, and reached that island on the 17th of November, most of her crew being by that time convalescent. The "Albert" continued her voyage up the Niger on the very day that the "Wilberforce" started for the coast. Her condition was far from encouraging. Only six Europeans among her crew were fit for duty, and before night even some of those began to complain of illness. Among the number was Captain Bird Allen, who had so gallantly left his ship in command of a junior officer, that he might remain with the expedition, and give all the assistance he could to Captain Trotter. "Thus," says Mr. Schön, "our hopes of advancing and accomplishing our objects are again involved in clouds of uncertainty. On the 23rd of September, the "Albert" had reached Gori, where an interesting incident occurred.

A large canoe coming down the river came alongside the steamer, and curious to inspect a vessel of her size, the owner of the canoe went on board. The canoe contained three slaves, two women and a man. The owner, a man named Aggiddi, when asked to bring the slaves on board the "Albert" did so, not at all suspecting the danger he was running. He acknowledged that he had bought the slaves the day before at Egga. Captain Trotter, on hearing the story, immediately resolved to liberate the slaves, on the ground that Aggiddi was one of the subjects of the King of Iddah, who seventeen days before had entered into a treaty to abolish the slave trade throughout his dominions; and that there had been sufficient time allowed for the publication of the treaty. Aggiddi pleaded ignorance of the treaty, but his plea was not allowed to prevent the liberation of the slaves. In consideration, however, of his having acted without a full knowledge of the consequences, and his candour in stating where he had procured the slaves, he was allowed the full price which he had paid for them, and none of the goods in his canoe were confiscated, as they might have been, according to the terms of the treaty.

Captain Trotter gave names to the slaves. The

man he called Albert Gori; one of the women Hannah Buxton, and the other Elizabeth Fry. When the women first came on board tears rolled down their cheeks, and they sat down not venturing to raise their eyes. One of them had been in slavery for three years; her own husband being jealous of her had sold her, and since then she had been sold nine times, and carried from place to place. No doubt they thought that they had fallen into worse hands than ever they had been in before, when they found themselves on board a British ship of war, surrounded by white men. They were soon, however, made to understand by means of an interpreter that they were quite safe, and that they had been made free. They had wholesome food and decent clothing given to them, and their faces soon showed that they fully appreciated the kindness that had been bestowed on them.

Egga was the next station of the "Albert." There Captain Trotter sent an embassy to the Chief, consisting of Dr. Stanger and Mr. Schön. He was asked to use his influence for the suppression of the slave trade, and replied that he was willing to do so, but that probably nothing would be done until Sumo Sariki, the Supreme Chief, had decided on his course of action. He afterwards said that he thought it probable that Sumo Sariki would enter into a treaty, as other chiefs had done, and would abide by its conditions so long as the British vessels were at hand, but that as soon as they were withdrawn he would commit ravages with redoubled fury.

Mr. Schön found Egga even more unhealthy, and therefore more unsuitable for a missionary station than Iddah. "Having now advanced," he says, "upwards of three hundred miles into the interior in search of comparatively healthier stations than those along the coast, and being obliged to sum up my investigations in this single sentence, 'I have seen none,' I feel no small portion of grief and sorrow, especially when I consider that the people, to all appearances, would be ready to receive the gospel of our salvation with open arms and hearts."

It was Captain Trotter's intention to ascend still higher up the river, and if possible to reach Rabba; but on the 4th of October he was compelled to order a return to the coast without delay. Captain Bird Allen was still very ill. Captain Trotter himself felt some symptoms of fever; and there was only one European officer on board fit for duty. A message was sent to the king of Rabba, to the effect that Commissioners from the Queen of England had intended to visit his country, but that they had been prevented partly by illness and partly by the falling of the river, and adding that they hoped to be able to return next season to confer with him on several important matters. A drawing of the three vessels forming the expedition was sent to him, with a rich velvet cloak and a handsomely-bound Arabic Bible. He was also informed that an English settlement had been formed at Adda Kuddu, and he was requested not to allow his warriors to come near the settlement.

Five days after, the "Albert" anchored at the Confluence: and ten days later, on the 13th of October, arrived at the sea-coast. A wonderful change for the better took place in the invalids as soon as the ship was once more at sea. On Sunday, October the 17th, at four in the afternoon, the "Albert" cast anchor at Fernando Po. The cool and refreshing sea-breeze, which the fever-stricken patients inhaled there, soon restored most of them to perfect health. Some, however, were too far gone to recover. Eight of them closed their earthly career at Fernando Po, and were buried near the resting-place of Mr. Richard Lander, the zealous African traveller. Amongst these was Captain Bird Allen, who fell a victim to his conscientious regard to duty.

I cannot forbear quoting in this place what Mr. Schön says of the last moments of this truly excellent man:—" Captain B. Allen," he says, "expired on the 25th of October, at ten o'clock, a.m., and was buried by myself late in the evening of the same day. Of him it can be said with perfect truth, 'To live is Christ, to die is gain.' His patience under sufferings, his resignation to the will of God, and his firm but humble assurance of his acceptance with God through Jesus Christ, made his position truly enviable, and demanded from all who witnessed him the sincere prayer, 'Let my last end be like his.' With him fell another victim to the cause of Africa, but it was a free-will offering to Him 'who gave Himself a ransom for all.' I spent many an hour by his bed-side reading the Word of God to him, in which he always felt great delight, and commending him in prayer to the care and mercy of Almighty God. His humility, his faith in God's Word, his love unfeigned, his tender concern for every one in the expedition, and especially for his companions in tribulation, his mild and charitable judgment in all things, will, I trust, be ever before my eyes, as worthy of imitation."

I have briefly related, without, however, omitting any important circumstance, the history of the Niger Expedition. Let us now see whether it was attended with any beneficial results.

Mr. Schön, writing on the 10th of October, when the "Albert" was on her return voyage down the river, says:—"It seems to be my task at present to look at things as they occur, and to draw inferences from them which may assist in the arrangement of future measures. The former I will do as long as I can. I will record as much as I am able. The inferences, however, I consider best to postpone. At present I can only come to one conclusion; and the result of the expedition seems to be summed up in this single sentence—*it has failed.* Not in its primary objects—forming treaties with the kings, and abolishing the slave-trade—but as the result of all the information I have obtained shows, that no commercial intercourse between the interior of Africa and England will unite the two countries, and so facilitate that access for which missionaries are looking and longing; and that the extreme unhealthiness of the river will ever prove a great barrier to all the undertakings on its banks of European agents."

Subsequent experience, however, showed that the expedition had not failed. It had unfortunately been attended with great loss of life, forty-two deaths having taken place, and it had not been the means of adding to the material wealth of our country by opening up Africa to the enterprise of our merchants and traders. Neither had it advanced in any perceptible degree the interests of religion amongst the people of Africa. And yet it had been attended with good results.

There were many in England who said very harsh things of the Ministers of State who had planned and sent out the expedition, and who called the men engaged in it "misguided men." In Parliament the Government was called to account for advising Her Majesty to send out the expedition; but there were not wanting able men to justify the course that had been taken. Amongst others, Sir Robert Inglis defended the action of the Government, and spoke of the men who were engaged in the expedition as "men who were exceeded in gallantry by none engaged in the service of their country." The expedition had *not failed*.

In the first place, several of the chiefs living on the banks of the Niger had had the British nation and British character presented to them in a new light. Up to that time they had only known the subjects of Queen Victoria as men engaged in the slave trade. Now they heard that only a few cruel and unprincipled men engaged in it; that the nation had long given it up, and was anxious to suppress it altogether. They recognised in the visitors to their country men who were anxious to be their friends and benefactors, who, at a great sacrifice of life and money, had come amongst them solely to promote their benefit, by establishing lawful commerce, and encouraging agriculture, in the place of the baneful and hated traffic in human beings.

But, in addition to all this, treaties had been actually concluded between the commissioners and some of the native chiefs, who bound themselves, under penalty of incurring the displeasure of the British Government, to carry out the objects for which the expedition had been planned. A foundation had been thus laid for future efforts in the same direction.

The expedition was, moreover, the means of making our countrymen better acquainted than they had been with the languages and dialects of the tribes who lived on the banks of the Niger, and in the interior of Africa. This was a matter of great importance, for before religious instruction could be imparted to the natives, it was absolutely necessary that their languages should be learned, and reduced to writing by Europeans.

The intercourse carried on by the commissioners with the native chiefs served, too, to impress their minds with the superiority which knowledge gave to the white man. They desired especially to learn to read the "White Man's Book," and to receive religious teachers from our countrymen. An important step in advance was gained for future missionaries.

Another result of the expedition was the proof which it supplied of the willingness of the chiefs to receive religious instruction, even from *black* men, if they considered them competent to impart instruction. This is a fact of the greatest importance, in its bearing on the spread of Christianity in Africa, because the expedition showed clearly that European agency cannot be successfully employed to any great extent for the accomplishment of that great work.

The expedition, by establishing clearly the fact

that if Africa is to be Christianized, it must be by natives, has strengthened the obligation to train natives to become religious teachers of their countrymen. The Church Missionary Society has been foremost in this good work of training a body of native clergymen, schoolmasters, and catechists, who are at this moment actively employed in promoting the welfare of their countrymen. So that, although the Niger Expedition may be said to have to some extent failed, yet it was not altogether unattended by beneficial results.

It led, beyond all question, to the establishment of the Niger mission as an offshoot from that at Sierra Leone, and to the appointment of Bishop Crowther as the first overseer of a work calculated to impart invaluable blessings to Africa.

Captain Trotter had shown that difficult and dangerous as it was to ascend the Niger it was not impossible. Brave men followed in his footsteps, and fourteen years after, in 1855, a screw steamer, the "Pleiad," fitted out by Mr. McGregor Laird, entered the Niger, and not only reached the Confluence, but taking the right hand branch, the Tshadda which flows from the East, succeeded in penetrating 300 miles further than any European had gone before, and that without any loss of life. Two years after, Mr. Laird entered into a contract with Her Majesty's Government to carry on the exploration of the interior of Africa by the Niger and its tributaries for five years. Thus a systematic attempt was made to introduce into Central Africa the blessings of Christianity and the blessings of commercial intercourse.

Mr. Crowther accompanied by several native teachers joined Laird's expedition in 1857. We shall see in our next chapter, that it was in that year that the Niger mission was established, and a great experiment successfully carried out in the face of much opposition and many sinister forebodings.

"Whatever methods," says Sir T. F. Buxton, "may be attempted for ameliorating the condition of untutored man, Christianity alone can penetrate to the root of the evil, can teach him to love and befriend his neighbour, and cause him to act as a candidate for a higher and holier state of being.

"The hope, therefore, of effecting Africa's civilization and of inducing her tribes to relinquish the trade in man, is without this assistance, utterly vain. This mighty lever, when properly applied, can alone overturn the iniquitous systems which prevail throughout that continent. Let missionaries and schoolmasters, the plough and the spade go together, and agriculture will flourish; the avenues to legitimate commerce will be opened; confidence between man and man will be inspired; whilst civilization will advance as the natural effect, and Christianity operate as the proximate cause of this happy change."

CHAPTER VIII.

AFRICA'S BLACK BISHOP.

"Sow trustingly. Can ought ye do e'er fail
To meet His eye? He loves to bless
The scattered seed—sow on. Doth doubt assail?
The fruit will prove His faithfulness."—ANON.

SAMUEL CROWTHER, whose name has been frequently mentioned in the course of the foregoing narrative—the Bishop of the Niger—is a native of Oshogun, a small inland African village, about a hundred miles from the coast of Benin. Adjai was the name which he bore when a heathen.

One morning, in the spring of the year 1821, the sun rose as brightly as usual on the village, and the peaceful inhabitants of Oshogun began to prepare for their daily labour, little dreaming of the calamities which were to befall them before the sun again disappeared beneath the western horizon.

Adjai's family consisted that morning of his father and mother, two little sisters, a young cousin, and himself, at that time about eleven years of age. His mother was engaged in preparing breakfast, when suddenly an alarm was raised. The Eyo Mohammedans were marching towards the town, and were about to attack the inhabitants, and carry as many as they could seize into slavery. The men instantly seized their bows and arrows, and prepared to resist the invaders. The women collected all their little ones around them, and with as much baggage as they could carry, sought some place of safety. But before any place of shelter could be found, the Eyos surrounded the village, and after a few hours' hard fighting with the men of Oshogun, the gates were forced, and the enemy took possession of the place. Adjai's father seeing that longer resistance was useless, rushed into his hut, urged his wife to flee without delay, taking the children with her, and returning to his post amongst the armed men, was never seen again by any member of his family. The village was soon after set on fire. Adjai, with his mother, his sisters, and his cousin, were made captives, cords were tied round their necks, and they were driven away from their quiet home. Before they had got half way through the town, some Foulahs, who formed part of the invading army, took possession of Adjai's cousin, and he was separated from the rest of the party.

For twenty long miles they were driven like cattle along the road, until they reached a town called Isehin. Mothers and children, husbands and wives, brothers and sisters, toiled on, all bound together, beneath a blazing sun, and suffering intensely from hunger and thirst. About sunset, they reached a spring of water, and were allowed to drink. A little parched corn was all that was given them to eat; and at midnight they arrived at their destination.

On the following morning, the cords having been removed from their necks, they were presented to the chief of the Eyo tribe by their captors. The division of the spoil was then made; and tremblingly each family awaited the decision which was to separate the individual members from one another, perhaps for ever. Adjai and one of his sisters became the property of the chief. His mother, with his younger sister, were claimed by another victor. Later in the day he was exchanged for a horse; and thus, within the space of twenty-four hours, Adjai was torn from his home, separated from his parents and sisters, and cast on the world a miserable, heart-broken slave.

"From this period," he says in a touching letter to the Rev. William Jowett, written in 1837, "I must date the unhappy, but which I am now taught, in other respects, to call blessed day, which I shall never forget in my life. I call it *unhappy* day, because it was the day in which I was violently turned out of my father's house, and separated from my relations; and in which I was made to experience what is called to be in slavery:—with regard to its being called *blessed*, it being the day which Providence had marked out for me to set out on my journey from the land of heathenism, superstition, and vice, to a place where His gospel is preached."

The horse for which Adjai was exchanged did not suit, and in two months was returned to its former owner. Adjai, therefore, returned to the chief who had bartered him away, and was taken to a town called Dadda. Here he met again his mother and younger sister. His elder sister he never saw again. For three months he was employed at Dadda in cutting grass for horses, and he was sometimes allowed to see his mother. He even ventured to indulge the hope that he would never be separated from her again.

"At last," he says in his letter to Mr. Jowett, "an unhappy evening arrived when I was sent with a man to get some money at a neighbouring house. I went, but with some fears for which I could not account, and, to my great astonishment, in a few minutes I was added to the number of many other captives enfettered, to be led to the market-town early the next morning."

Adjai was conveyed, with his companions in slavery, to the town of Ijaye, a few days' journey from Dadda. There he was sold to a Mohammedan woman, with whom he travelled from place to place, visiting several towns, and settling down for three months at a place called Toko.

Occasionally Adjai's mistress spoke of going to the Popo country, and, as it was well known that the Portuguese often bought their slaves there, Adjai could not but fear that this portended further misery to him. This fear so preyed upon him, that he lost his appetite, and became very ill—so ill that he gave up all thoughts of happiness in this world, and deliberately contemplated suicide, as the only way of escape from the wretchedness which seemed on all sides to threaten him. But God, who had purposes of love in store for Adjai, and a work for him to do, still watched over his life, though he knew it not, and suffered him to do himself no harm.

His health having greatly failed, and his mistress beginning to fear that he might die, hastily sold him, and his price having been counted out before his eyes, he was handed over to a new owner, and taken away to a town called Jabbo.

From Jabbo, Adjai was removed to a slave-market called Ikosi, near the coast, and on the banks of a large river, which he supposes to have been the lagoon near Lagos. The sight of the water terrified him; and his alarm was greatly increased when he was ordered to enter the lagoon, and wade to a canoe which lay at a short distance from the shore, and which was to convey him to the opposite bank. He trembled all over as he prepared to obey his orders, and so slowly and cautiously did he put one foot before the other, that the men who had charge of him, having no time to spare, lifted him up, carried him to the canoe, and laid him down on some bags of corn. There he lay motionless and speechless for some hours, until Eko, on the opposite side of the lagoon, was reached.

At Eko, Adjai was allowed a good deal of liberty, his owner knowing that it was useless for him to attempt to escape, as the whole breadth of the lagoon lay between him and the open country. After remaining there for three months, he was sold to a Portuguese, and became for the first time the property of a white man. Other slaves shared his fate. The Portuguese were making their purchases for shipment across the Atlantic. "Men and boys," he says, "were at first chained together with a chain of about six fathoms in length, thrust through an iron fetter on the neck of every individual, and fastened at both ends with padlocks. In this situation the boys suffered most; the men sometimes getting angry, would draw the chain so violently, as seldom went without bruises on their poor little necks, especially the time to sleep, when they drew the chain so close, to ease themselves of its weight, in order to be able to lie more conveniently, that we were almost suffocated, or bruised to death, in a room with one door, which was fastened as soon as we entered in, with no other passage for communicating the air than the openings under the eavesdrop. Very often at night, when two or three individuals quarrelled or fought, the whole drove suffered punishment without any distinction. At last we boys had the happiness to be separated from the men when their number was increased, and no more chain to spare; we were corded together by ourselves."

This state of things lasted for four months. At last the time for embarkation came. One hundred and eighty-seven unhappy prisoners were put on board of a slave-ship, which started from Lagos for her voyage across the Atlantic. The slave-dealers, however, had been watched. On the very next evening after that on which the ship sailed, two English men-of-war bore down upon her, and without much difficulty she was captured. Adjai had the satisfaction of seeing the Portuguese captain, and all his crew, made prisoners, whilst he and his companions in slavery regained their liberty. The ships of war were the "Myrmidon," Captain H. J. Leeke, and the "Iphigenia," Captain Sir Robert Mends. The date of the capture was the 7th of April, 1822.

Adjai and six of his companions were transferred to the "Myrmidon." The first object that attracted their attention was part of a dead pig, suspended over the deck, which they believed to be human flesh, never having seen raw pork before. On looking round them, they saw what they took to be negroes' heads, piled up most carefully, but which proved, on closer examination, to be cannon balls.

Their fears were soon allayed. They discovered, to their great delight, that they were not amongst slave-dealers and cannibals, but amongst honourable, brave, and Christian men, who were there for the very purpose of delivering them from cruel bondage. They were supplied with decent clothes, and made to do light work on board the ship.

After cruising about for two months and a half, Adjai and his young companions were landed at Sierra Leone, on the 17th of June, 1822: and on the same day they were sent, with about thirty other boys, to Bathurst, about seven miles from Freetown. Here, to their great delight, they met many of their countrymen, who, like themselves, had been liberated from slavery, and they were assured that slavery was impossible within the British dominions. They were free, and under no apprehension of being again made slaves.

The British officers who were the instruments of restoring Adjai to liberty, had discharged their duty when they landed him safely on the hospitable shores of Sierra Leone. Thenceforth he was to be under the care of that noble Christian Society which had already done so much for Africa. He was placed in a mission school in which there were about 200 boys and girls; and a black monitor was appointed to teach him the alphabet. Intelligent and anxious to learn, he soon mastered the first difficulties in the art of reading; and in order to encourage him the missionary's wife gave him special instructions, together with a little native girl named Asano, who had also given proofs of superior intelligence, and who belonged to the same tribe as Adjai. For three years Adjai diligently attended school, and when he had been sufficiently instructed in the Christian faith, and had given proof of the depth and sincerity of his religious belief, he was baptized on the 11th of December, 1825. He now renounced his heathen name, and received that of a well-known English clergyman, Samuel Crowther. He has since done much to render the name very memorable in the annals of West Africa.

The year after he was baptized he was sent for a short time to England. He would willingly have prolonged his stay, in order to make himself acquainted with the many wonderful things which formed such a contrast to what he had been accustomed to in his African home. But it was considered advisable by his friends that he should return to Sierra Leone, and there prepare himself for his future work. The Fourah Bay Institution, of which mention has already been made, had just been opened, and he was admitted to it as the first student. There he received that full measure of Christian instruction for which he had ardently longed; and there he learned that the service of Christ is indeed perfect freedom. In the year 1829, he was married to a Christian woman, who a few years before had been the little girl who received her early instruction with him from the lips of a missionary's wife. She too had renounced her heathen name Asano, had been baptized, and had received the name Susanna.

For many years after he left the Fourah Bay Institution, Crowther toiled energetically and successfully as a schoolmaster at Regent's Town, the scene, as I have already said, of Mr. Johnson's labours. But useful and successful as he was there, God had higher work for him to do.

We have seen what an active part he took in carrying out the objects of the first Niger Expedition. He was happily preserved amidst all the danger and the fearful mortality which cut down many of his associates. He returned in safety to his family, with his desire to benefit his native country deepened, and with the earnest wish that since it had pleased God to disappoint the efforts made by Europeans to introduce the gospel of the Divine Saviour into the interior of Africa, the sons of Africa themselves might receive such instruction as should qualify them to become missionaries to their own countrymen.

His desire was granted. He himself was the first who was selected for this glorious work. He visited England a second time, and was admitted as a student into the Church Missionary Society's

College, at Islington. Those who knew him there can testify that his consistent conduct and Christian demeanour made him beloved by his tutors as well as by his fellow students. When his course of study was completed, having given full proof of his thorough fitness for the work to which he was called, he was ordained by the Bishop of London.

Few can realize the emotions of the once miserable African slave boy, as he felt the Bishop's hand laid upon his head, and heard the solemn words pronounced:—"Take thou authority to preach the Word of God, and to minister the holy Sacraments in the congregations where thou shalt be lawfully appointed thereunto." Then he saw more clearly than he had ever seen before, the mercy and the grace which had separated him in childhood from his heathen home, not only that he himself might know and love the Saviour, but that he might become the ambassador of that Saviour to his dark but still beloved land.

He returned to Sierra Leone as the Rev. Samuel Crowther; but the scene of his labours was not to be the colony which had been already christianized by the labours of European missionaries. He was to carry the glad tidings of salvation to other regions as yet untrodden by the feet of Christ's messengers.

The Yoruba tribes who had formerly lived in scattered villages, had determined to band themselves together for mutual protection from the incursions of slave dealers, and to found a new city to which they gave the name of Abbeokuta. Before long about 70,000 inhabitants took up their abode within the city. Accompanied by Mr. Townsend and Mr. Gollmer in 1844, Crowther left Sierra Leone for Abbeokuta by way of Badagry. The ship which conveyed them to Badagry had once been a slaver, but had become the property of a Christian African merchant of one of the Yoruba tribes who had himself once been a slave. With money honestly earned in business he had purchased the vessel, and had named it the "Wilberforce." In this vessel he offered a free passage to the missionary party. Thus the first heralds of Christian liberty to the Yoruba country were carried thither in a captured slave ship by a liberated slave.

Being detained for many months at Badagry by the news that war had broken out in the Yoruba territory, Crowther employed his time in translating into his native language portions of the Bible; and before long he completed the Gospel according to St. Luke, the Acts of the Apostles, and the Epistle of St. Paul to the Romans, so that the people might learn in their own tongue "the wonderful works of God." On the 27th of July, 1846, Mr. Townsend and Mr. Crowther started for Abbeokuta. Mr. Gollmer, whose wife as I have already related, died at Badagry, remained behind for a time. Nothing could be more affectionate than their reception by the chief Sodeke and his people. Two months after an event occurred which filled him with wonder and with joy. I relate it in his own words. "The text for this day," the 21st of August, 1846—he says, "in the Christian almanack is, 'Thou art the helper of the fatherless.' I have never felt the force of this text more than I have this day, as I have to relate that my mother, from whom I was torn away about five and twenty years ago, came with my brother in search of me. When she saw me she trembled. She could not believe her own eyes. We grasped one another, looking at each other with silence and great astonishment; big tears rolled down her emaciated cheeks. She trembled as she held me by the hand, and called me by the familiar names by which I well remember I used to be called by my grandmother, who has since died in slavery. We could not say much, but sat still and cast now and then an affectionate look at each other—a look which violence and oppression had long checked;—an affection which had nearly been extinguished by the long space of twenty-five years. Thus unsought for, after all search for me had failed, God has brought us together again, and turned our sorrow into joy."

Crowther's mother had passed through much affliction during those twenty-five years. The greater part of the time had been spent in slavery. She had for five years lived as a slave in Abbeokuta, at the end of which time she had been redeemed by her daughters, who collected the requisite sum of money. As soon as she was set at liberty, she went to live with her daughters, and took care of their children, at a place called Abaka, near Abbeokuta, and it was whilst there that she heard tidings of her long lost son, and went to Abbeokuta to meet him.

Crowther was soon eagerly engaged in his missionary work. Young and old, rich and poor, chiefs and people, listened attentively to his instruction. A church was built and a considerable congregation collected. Neat houses, too, were built for the missionaries, which were the wonder of all the natives, who seeing how different they were from their own rude huts, confessed that "white man had sense;" and both chiefs and people often spent hours in looking at them and admiring them. In the course of time a little band of natives, who had renounced idolatry, offered themselves for Christian baptism. Amongst these was Afala, Crowther's mother. She received the appropriate name of Hannah.

On the 3rd of August, 1849, Crowther writes:— "This mission is to-day three years old; and if we look back during that period we have much cause for thankfulness for the protecting care of our

Heavenly Father in the midst of superstitious enemies, who would have swallowed us up, or driven us from the field. What has God wrought during this short interval of conflict between light and darkness? At the lowest calculation we have 500 constant attendants on the means of grace, about 80 communicants, and nearly 200 candidates for Baptism and the Lord's Supper."

The general results of the Abbeokuta mission are briefly alluded to in Chapter VI. The part which Crowther took in the work was such as to draw to him the attention of all the friends of missionary enterprise. He was again summoned to England, and his simple and touching accounts of what had been done in West Africa, together with his own romantic history, excited universal interest.

He soon, however, returned to Africa, and continued his labours in the Yoruba country, not scorning even the elementary work of teaching very young children their alphabet, and their first lessons in reading.

The Church Missionary Society now determined to try the experiment of establishing a mission on the Niger in which only native clergymen and schoolmasters should be employed, the climate having been found, as I have already said, utterly unsuitable to the constitutions of Europeans. Accordingly Crowther, with another native clergyman, and five native lay assistants, in 1857 joined the third expedition conducted by Mr. McGregor Laird, and mission stations were formed at Onitsha, at Gbebe near the confluence, and at Rabba on the Quorra branch of the Niger.

Ever since its first commencement the Niger mission has been conducted by Africans, and has prospered in spite of special difficulties which are unknown in Sierra Leone and in every other country which has the happiness to possess a settled government. Seven years of unremitting toil seemed to strengthen the confidence which Crowther had already inspired; and as it was most important that the native church on the Niger should be properly organized and made independent, it was resolved to appoint a Bishop, under whose jurisdiction all the native clergy should be placed. No one could have been found more suitable for the office than Crowther. He seems indeed to have been raised up by Providence for this very purpose. His previous history, his training, his talents, all assisted to qualify him for the honourable though arduous post of Bishop of the Niger.

On the 29th of June, 1864, Crowther having again visited England, was consecrated in Canterbury Cathedral, the Bishops of Peterborough (Dr. Jeune) and of Tasmania (Dr. Bromby) being consecrated with him. The interest excited by the consecration of an African in England was very great. Hundreds of persons were assembled in the choir, nave, and aisles of the cathedral, although very few out of the number were able either to see or hear what was going on. Amongst those who were present in the cathedral was the benevolent European lady, the missionary's wife, who had first taught him his letters and had given him Christian advice and instruction immediately after his liberation from the slave ship. To her more than to anybody else the contrast between Adjai the slave and Crowther the Bishop, must have appeared indeed striking. She had "cast her bread upon the waters," and she had found it "after many days."

Just before his consecration the University of Oxford conferred on him the honorary degree of Doctor of Divinity.

Bishop Crowther, as we must now call him, returned to Africa about a month after his elevation to the episcopate, followed by the prayers of many of his European friends that he might, in the words of the consecration service, "have grace evermore to be ready to spread abroad the gospel, and as a wise and faithful servant, giving to Christ's family their portion in due season, at last be received into everlasting joy."

He reached Lagos on the 22nd of August, and on the 24th he admitted the Rev. Lambert McKenzie to priest's orders. Then he ascended the Niger on board the "Investigator," which was bound to the confluence with supplies for Dr. Baikie. This gave him an opportunity of visiting the stations already established, and forming plans for the planting of new ones; after which he returned to Sierra Leone for a fresh supply of native teachers to strengthen and enlarge the church of which he had been appointed chief pastor.

In 1867 an incident occurred which was nearly attended with fatal consequences to the Bishop and his staff of Christian teachers. He had accomplished the ascent of the Niger as far as the confluence, and was on his return journey, when, hearing that a chief with whom he had been on friendly terms for twenty years, was encamped on the bank of the river, he landed to exchange friendly salutations with him. Without any warning, and without any reason being assigned, the Bishop was seized and made prisoner. A large sum was then demanded for his ransom. But when the news of his capture reached the confluence, both Europeans and natives determined to rescue the Bishop for whom they felt great regard, and not to encourage similar acts by consenting to pay for his release. They immediately descended the river, landed where the Bishop was detained, and endeavoured by remonstrances with the chief to obtain his liberty; but finding him obstinate, they snatched the Bishop from him by main force, and retreated to their vessel, defending themselves as they retreated. An arrow unhappily struck Mr. Fell, British Vice-Consul at Lokoja, and he died of the wound a few hours after. The Bishop's life was, however, saved by his gallantry, and probably the safety of all the mission stations along the Niger ensured ; for if this hostile chief had succeeded in extorting a ransom for the Bishop, others doubtless would have followed his example.

In recounting and commenting upon this incident, the Bishop says :—" In taking a retrospective view of the past year, we see throughout it a mysterious hand of Providence upon Africa, the movements of which we cannot understand. In the midst of apparently encouraging success to persevere in pushing forward the long-made arduous efforts to explore the continent, to discover its internal facilities and resources, with the two-fold noble object in view of introducing legitimate trade in the place of traffic in a fellow man, and of planting Christianity with its attendant blessings, in the room of heathenish superstition and its numberless accompanying evils, a gloom is permitted to be cast over the face of these laudable attempts, as if Africa were doomed to perpetual isolation, and to be barred out from intercourse with the civilized world, as if she were bent on self destruction and everlasting debasement, through the abominable slave trade, by acting, through ignorance, in direct opposition to the best wishes and pious and benevolent labours of her best friends."

Anxious to imitate his episcopal brethren in England, Bishop Crowther on the occasion of his third visit to the Niger, assembled as many of his native clergy and lay teachers as he could conveniently get together, and delivered to them a charge at Lokoja station near the confluence. He mentions this in a letter written by him to the Archbishop of Canterbury, and adds:—"By thus digesting such parts of the Holy Scriptures bearing on the subject of the working of Christian missionaries amongst the heathen, we may be better guided and more encouraged in our efforts to introduce Christianity among them."

Bishop Crowther's work on the Niger has now been carried on for ten years with varying success. He has five stations under his superintendence—Onitsha, Akassa, Lokoja, Bonny, and Brass. The number of native clergy at present is only eight, and of unordained teachers twelve; but the work in which the Bishop is engaged possesses the power of expansion as circumstances dictate. To ordain more clergymen until they are required and can be supported, would be absurd; but as congregations are gathered from amongst the heathen the Bishop will ordain and appoint pastors over them. One of his own sons—the Rev. Dandeson Coates

Crowther—has been appointed to Bonny, where the native congregation now exceeds one hundred.

I cannot better conclude this chapter than in the words in which Bishop Crowther describes an ordination which he held at Bonny church, on Trinity Sunday, May 26th, 1872. After describing the arrangements in the church, he says:—" I was just concluding my sermon, when nearly all the chiefs of Bonny made their appearance. I stood still till they were all seated; the last part of my sermon being more applicable to them, as it treated of baptism, the last commission from Christ to His Apostles, I begged the patience of the congregation to preach the last four pages a second time, for the benefit of late comers, which I did: all kept their places, and listened with patience and much attention. I at the same time acknowledged the liberal pecuniary aid received from different individuals to encourage them in the habit of self-support to which they are being trained. After the sermon the ordination took place. It was to them a novel sight to see how Christians set apart their priests for the service of God. The three candidates, the three assisting priests, and the bishop, neatly apparelled nearly all in white, with deep solemnity going through the ceremony of the whole service, was a sight quite different from their heathenish practices: no violent gestures, no vociferations, no repulsive sights to the human feelings of remains of human bodies, such as skulls and bones, of limbs strung in rows, with which the temples are decorated, are to be seen at *our* place of worship. No! instead of this there is an airy, neat church, proper seats are provided, silence and order are kept throughout, prayers are offered to God our Creator for friends and enemies in the name of the Son our Redeemer, and of the Holy Ghost our Sanctifier, who willeth all men to be saved and to come to the knowledge of the truth. Four hundred and sixty-nine natives and seven Europeans were present at church at the morning service."

Surely no one will say after reading these words, that missionary labour on the Niger has been fruitless. No one who, ever so little, appreciates the efforts made by Bishop Crowther and his Christian fellow-countrymen will deny that the words of the prophet Isaiah may not unaptly be applied to the inhabitants of the country watered by the great river Niger and its tributaries:—"The people that walked in darkness have seen a great light; they that dwell in the land of the shadow of death, upon them hath the light shined."

CHAPTER IX.

THE VICTORY OF FAITH.

"From all Thy saints in warfare, for all Thy saints at rest,
To Thee, O blessed Jesu, all praises be addressed.
Thou, Lord, didst win the battle, that they might conquerors be;
Their crowns of living glory are lit with rays from Thee."

NELSON.

"THE social advancement of Sierra Leone," says the Sixty-Seventh Annual Report of the Church Missionary Society, "is the triumph of a great philanthropic and religious enterprize."

The facts related in the preceding pages go far to prove the correctness of the foregoing statement.

There are, it is true, some who have visited Sierra Leone, who have denied the success of the experiment, so far as the religious and social elevation of the people is concerned. The accounts given by missionaries, or those interested in missionary societies, are objected to by some parties as being partial and exaggerated reports of their achievements; although all who know the truth of the case bear testimony that missionaries far oftener understate than exaggerate the result of their labours.

It is therefore satisfactory to be able to say that there is ample evidence of the truth of the statements made in the foregoing chapters to be found in the report of a Parliamentary Select Committee, which sat during the session of 1865, to investigate the condition of the West African colonies. That Committee was eminently impartial in its composition, and examined witnesses notoriously hostile to the negro race and to Christian missions, as well as those who were favourable. The Committee, at the close of its investigations, presented to the House the evidence they had received, together with a few recommendations. These documents have been printed in a Blue Book. They are too voluminous to quote here, but they are accessible to the public, and they may be appealed to without any hesitation as establishing the main facts which the Church Missionary Society has from year to year reported in proof of the social and religious progress of the liberated Africans and their descendants in Sierra Leone.

Her Majesty's Government had sent out, in 1864, a special commissioner, Colonel Ord, of the Royal Engineers, Governor of Bermuda, to visit and report upon the four colonies of West Africa, which he had on a former occasion officially inspected. Colonel Ord was examined before the Committee, and one passage, which states the conclusion of his investigations, is as follows:—" So far as the suppression of the slave trade and the encouragement of commerce are concerned, it may be said that the settlements satisfactorily attain the principal objects for which they are maintained; but it must be borne in mind that there are other objects, the attainment of which augments greatly the advantages which the maintenance of the settlement confers: these are, the abolition of human sacrifice and other similar barbarous practices, the removal of that oppression and injustice which too often attend the administration of native laws, and the introduction of such modifications into the laws and customs regarding domestic slaves, as shall at least lead to some improvement in their condition, if it does not altogether free them from bondage. There has been spread widely abroad an appreciation of the superiority of European civilization, and of the advantages it brings with it, the results of which, if not yet apparent, there can be no doubt will be seen hereafter."

In the year 1852 an important event occurred in the history of the Sierra Leone Church. Her first Bishop, the Right Rev. Dr. Vidal, was appointed and consecrated in England. He landed at Freetown on the 26th of December. Dr. Vidal had been the rector of a small village in Sussex. He possessed a great talent for languages, and was led in a very remarkable way to study the Yoruba language. Although at the time that he was engaged in studying it no one could suppose it would ever be of any use to him; and, indeed, he himself seems to have regarded the language rather as a literary curiosity than an acquisition of any practical benefit; yet when Mr. Crowther was in England, making preparations for the publication of his Yoruba Dictionary, Dr. Vidal was able to be of immense service to him. His buried talent was exhumed, and applied to a most useful purpose; and some years after, when the Sierra Leone bishopric was founded, and those in whose gift the appointment lay looked about for a suitable man, the service rendered to the missionary cause by Dr. Vidal was brought to light, his knowledge of one of the native languages of Africa was made known, and he was accordingly selected as the first bishop of Sierra Leone.

Bishop Vidal spent the year 1853 in diligently inspecting every part of his diocese. He preached in season and out of season; he confirmed, he ordained, he gave sound advice to all who needed it, and he seemed to be the "right man in the right place." The native church flourished under his direction, and there were apparently many years of prosperity and happiness before him. His career, however, was destined to be a short one. In November, 1854, nearly two years after his arrival in the colony, the bishop visited the Yoruba country, and was there welcomed with great rejoicings by the native Christians. He confirmed, whilst there, six hundred candidates, and ordained two native pastors. The visit, full as it was of most interesting incidents, was yet a very solemn one. Several deaths had occurred from fever. The bishop must have inhaled the deadly poison, and carried the fever with him on board the steamer which was to convey him back to Freetown. Soon after the vessel left the coast the bishop was taken ill; he became worse and worse; and when the steamer entered the harbour, the flag floating at half-mast-high announced to the expectant people of Sierra Leone that only the lifeless body of Bishop Vidal had returned from the Yoruba country.

Two years after, Bishop Weeks was appointed to succeed him. He had been for twenty years a schoolmaster in West Africa, and when his health seemed to have been completely broken down by the climate, he returned to England. His native air having recruited his health, he sought and received ordination, and was appointed to a missionary cure in one of the most heathen districts of London. When, therefore, a successor to Bishop Vidal was sought, no fitter man could be found than the man who had successfully combated heathenism abroad as well as at home, and Mr. Weeks was consecrated and sent out to Sierra Leone.

He was welcomed back to the colony most warmly and affectionately. The people felt that in him they had a sympathizing friend, for he had dwelt so long in Africa that he could understand them far better than any stranger could have done. On Trinity Sunday, 1856, he ordained eight native pastors at Freetown; and then, like his predecessor, visited the Yoruba country. He was at Abbeokuta on Christmas Day, and congregations of native Christians from the different churches in that large city flocked around their bishop to welcome him, and to hear his words of holy counsel. There he met his old friend Mr. Crowther, who, like himself, was soon to be called to the office of a bishop in the Church of God.

He, too, breathed the fever-infected air of the Yoruba country. Like Bishop Vidal, he was taken ill on board the steamer that conveyed him home. On his arrival at Freetown he was carried ashore in his hammock, and taken to Fourah Bay. There, a few days after, he died. The second Bishop of Sierra Leone had been summoned away by his Divine Master, and rested from his labours.

A few months after the death of Bishop Weeks, his successor, Bishop Bowen, landed in the colony.

Dr. Bowen was a remarkable man. Possessed of a robust frame, a cheerful temperament, and great energy, he settled in early life in Canada, and devoted himself to farming; but being influenced by an irresistible desire to devote himself to the work of the Christian ministry, he gave up his secular calling, returned to Ireland, his native country, entered Trinity College, Dublin, and in due time obtained his degree, and was ordained. After serving for some time in a curacy, he offered his services to the Church Missionary Society, and travelled at his own expense, but under the control of the Committee, through Palestine, inspecting and reporting upon the missionary work.

He paid two separate visits to Palestine, and then settled down as a country pastor in England.

In 1857 he was offered and accepted the Bishopric of Sierra Leone. The following year the celebrated Dr. Livingstone visited the colony, and in a letter to Sir Roderick Murchison, dated March 30th, 1858, he said:—"We were here on Sunday last and saw an ordination service by the Bishop (Bowen), an energetic and good man. He was a missionary formerly, and a better man for a bishop could not have been selected. The Sunday is wonderfully observed; as well, I think, as anywhere in Scotland. Looking at the change effected among the people, and comparing the masses here with what we find at parts along the coast where the benign influence of Christianity have had no effect, 'the man' even 'who has no nonsense about him,' would be obliged to confess that England had done some good by her philanthropy, ay, and an amount of good that will look grand in the eyes of posterity."

It was hoped that Dr. Bowen's strong constitution would enable him to resist the climate and to live for many years to preside over the West African Church. Twice he was laid prostrate by the fever, and twice he recovered; but the third time even his physical strength gave way; and after filling his high office, for only two years, he was gathered unto his fathers.

Thus, in the short course of seven years three bishops had fallen victims to the deadly climate of West Africa.

In 1860 Dr. Beccles was appointed to fill the post left vacant by the death of Bishop Bowen. He is the only bishop whose life was spared for a period longer than that enjoyed by his predecessors. He lived not only to spend nine years in Sierra Leone, but to return to England where he now enjoys comparative rest as rector of a country parish.

It was during the episcopate of Bishop Beccles, in the year 1866, that the West African Church celebrated her jubilee.

The first note of the jubilee was sounded by the Bishop's sermon in the Cathedral at Freetown. He took for his text the closing words of St. Matthew's Gospel, in which the Saviour tells the little apostolic company that all power is given to

Him in heaven and on earth, bids them go and teach all nations, and promises to be with them always, even to the end of the world. The governor presided over the jubilee meeting, and expressed his conviction, the result of observation and experience, that the conversion and civilization of the inhabitants of the colony were due to the Church Missionary Society. A native clergyman acted as Secretary to the meeting, and in a powerful speech reviewed the last fifty years of missionary labour in the colony. He reminded his countrymen of the days when Africa—Northern Africa—gave martyrs to the flames and bishops to the church; he sketched the rise and progress of Moslem power, when cathedrals were converted into mosques, the Koran took the place of the Bible, and the Crescent supplanted the Cross. He related how in 1808 Sierra Leone became the home of liberated slaves, speaking more than a hundred different languages. He told how amongst this population, dissimilar in language, habits, and manners, the Church Missionary Society had laboured ever since the year 1816 with truly Christian zeal; and how, during the first ten years, one-half out of the twenty-eight missionaries who arrived in the colony died, the victims of an unhealthy climate.

Another African clergyman informed the meeting that of all the European labourers who arrived in Sierra Leone during the twenty years that elapsed between 1816 and 1836, only one—Mr. Townsend of Abbeokuta—was then alive and still engaged in missionary work. "But," he added, "a band of thirty-one native clergymen has arisen to occupy the places vacated by Europeans."

"The contrast" he continued "between the position of Christianity at the present time, and in 1816, speaks profitably and powerfully as to future missionary work." And commenting on his words the Committee of the Church Missionary Society said: "The sincere but faint-hearted friend, and the sceptical but fierce foe, may alike learn from the announcement made at the jubilee meeting in Sierra Leone, that while in 1816 the communicants of Western Africa had then only advanced to six, they are now advancing towards six thousand. Such is the blessed spiritual change effected within fifty years. The land of which it has been said that the slave trade has dyed its sands with blood, and charged every wind that floated over its plains with the sighs and groans of wretched murdered man, has so celebrated its missionary jubilee as to draw from our hearts the Psalmist's exclamation—'Happy are the people that are in such a case; yea, blessed are the people who have the Lord for their God.'"

I may here remark that the zeal of these African Christians did not expend itself in high-flown words or in mere declamation. They proved the earnestness of their purpose by contributing at the jubilee meeting the sum of £830; and they also erected during the year, at a cost of £900, three permanent churches in the heathen districts of Bullom and Sherbro.

The victory of faith was gained—a complete and real, though a bloodless victory—on the day on which the jubilee meeting was held.

The missionary history of Sierra Leone from that date to this, contains very much that is interesting, but not much that is either new or striking. It is no longer the history of assaults upon heathenism; but the record of the quiet unobtrusive work of the pastor amongst a Christian people.

Sierra Leone is not now so much a mission station as the head-quarters for the extension of African missions. The native church is firmly established. The voluntary contributions of the native Christians are steadily increasing. Connected with the native Pastorate there are now ten principal and eighteen subordinate stations. Each station has a substantial stone church, with a congregation varying from 200 to 700 persons. The self-supporting Grammar School, under the superintendence of an African clergyman, and containing a hundred African boys, continues to prosper. The Fourah Bay Institution sends out from time to time energetic pastors and teachers. The Female Institution, which provides an excellent education for girls of the higher classes, is well attended and generously supported. All the Christian machinery, indeed, which has been erected is kept in an efficient condition, and works on steadily and smoothly.

Vice and irreligion, however, still exist in Sierra Leone as elsewhere. The people, although greatly improved in morals, are very far from faultless. The visitor who expects to find there a condition of millenial peace and happiness, will be sadly disappointed. The evils of human nature have not been entirely removed. Christianity has produced in Sierra Leone results not differing very materially from those which it has produced in other countries. A general improvement has taken place. The worship of Jehovah has been substituted for the worship of idols. Christ is acknowledged as the God-Man, the Saviour of sinners. The influences of the Holy Spirit are not only believed in, but sought for. Large numbers of persons are doubtless sincere and earnest in their profession of the Christian religion ; and are actuated in all that they do by Christian principles. But, there are many more, whose religion is merely nominal ; and some perhaps, who regard religion as a convenient means of attaining worldly advancement and reputation.

Sierra Leone, however, is not worse, whether we consider the character of her people or the sincerity of their religious belief, than other Christian countries. Compared with herself in 1816 she is as different, as the genuine disciple of Christ is from the ferocious cannibal; or, as the civilized possessor of worldly wealth is, from the dejected and miserable slave. Compared with other countries in which the religion of Christ has become the religion of the masses, and in which there exist necessarily many hypocrites, Sierra Leone will certainly not suffer by the comparison.

The great object which the missionary is required to set before him, is the rescue of souls from the bondage of Satan. His great duty is to proclaim the fact of God's love to the world, manifested in the mission of His Son Jesus Christ. But subordinate to this duty, are others which the missionary ought to discharge, and, amongst these, one of the most important is the promotion of sound education.

We have seen what great efforts have been made to promote education in Sierra Leone, and we have also seen that the agents of the Church Missionary Society always took care to lay the foundation of the education which they imparted, deep in the knowledge of the Holy Scriptures. The result of their arduous labours is to be seen in the colony in the present day; but there, as elsewhere, a secularist party exists, which would educate without any reference to the Bible, or only such reference to it as might be made to any record of historical facts.

It is just as natural that this secularist party

should exist at Sierra Leone, as it is that it should exist in England, or in any other country where Christianity has become the religion of the multitude, but is believed in by comparatively very few. The same contest must be expected to be carried on there as elsewhere, on that most vital of all questions :—Is it possible to erect a sound educational structure, except on the foundation of true religion?

That education has made wonderful progress in Sierra Leone no one can doubt, who has read the newspapers published there, the letters and pamphlets of some of the leading native gentlemen of the colony, and the sermons of some of the native pastors. Even the most cursory reader of these papers, pamphlets, and sermons, will perceive that there is springing up a most natural and very proper feeling of independence and nationality. Whilst acknowledging the immense debt of gratitude due to Europeans, educated Africans are beginning to long to slip away from their European leading strings, and they are proving themselves perfectly capable of discharging all their duties as citizens and as Christians, without foreign aid.

In an article entitled "Christianity in Africa," which appeared in "The Negro," on the 3rd of May, 1873, reference is made to an address presented to the Rev. James Johnson, a native clergyman, with his reply. The writer says :—" The two documents reveal the conviction, as existing in the minds of all intelligent, educated, and thoughtful natives, that Africans are a distinct people from Europeans, and that European institutions, whether political or ecclesiastical, to take firm root among them, must be modified in their application, and adapted to the circumstances of the country."

And Mr. Johnson himself says:—"The desire to have an independent church closely follows the knowledge that we are a distinct race, existing under peculiar circumstances, and possessing peculiar characteristics. We desire to preserve this distinction uninjured, under the conviction that it would materially contribute to give a pure native character and power to our religious profession. The arrangements of foreign churches, made to suit their own local circumstances, can hardly be expected to suit our own in all their details."

Similar sentiments are expressed by gentlemen holding appointments under the colonial government.

Professor Blyden, an African gentleman, writing to the Governor, Mr. Pope Hennessy, on the proposal to establish a West African University, under date, December 6th, 1872, says:—"I do not deny that the creeds brought to us from Europe rest on certain deep convictions which are present to the consciousness of the people among whom they arose, and who now hold them, and I believe that they cover great truths; but I cannot see that these European formularies unmodified should be imposed upon Africa. They are instructive as records of religious growth and development in Europe, and may be of great suggestive use in guiding us in the development of the African church, which is sure to be formed in this country, if there be any natural or normal development. But it is evident, that to make these creeds, in all their details, authoritative in Africa, the intellectual and spiritual growth of the people must be checked or distorted, by the introduction of the bitterness of theological rancour, and the harshness of conflicting sects."

Professor Blyden ably argues in his letters, that Africans must be educated by Africans, and not by Europeans in future; and that the sentiments of race and nationality which certainly exist amongst negroes, must be cherished and fostered.

"To the Government of Sierra Leone," he says, "we look as the natural guardian of the people's interests, and the authorized disburser of the people's money, for purposes best promotive of the people's welfare; and if the Government receives the support of the natives of these settlements in the promotion of this work of education, it will be only aiding the Africans themselves to carry out a most important object, supplying themselves with educational means according to the providential laws of human growth, which must result in the moulding of a sober, well-disciplined, and efficient African character, set free from those influences which, hitherto, have as a general thing, only tended to crush or to stupify the intellect. And the dawn of a new era will be hastened, in which the Africans themselves, prepared by proper culture, will come forward as the actors and prominent figures in the great educational drama, to clench and rivet the nail driven by those of an alien race, who had the sagacity to perceive their needs, and the decision, energy, and benevolence, to act upon that perception."

The Church Missionary Society can hardly be expected to take a leading part in the promotion of merely secular schemes; but the views enunciated above, apply to spiritual as well as to secular matters. The West African Church, with its native pastors, is fast assuming the form, and acquiring the strength, of an independent national church, and it is right that the feeling of independence should be encouraged. The essential truths of the gospel are held in common by all churches which "are built upon the foundation of the apostles and prophets, Jesus Christ himself being the chief corner stone." But the mode of worship, and the internal government, must depend on the taste and character of each separate church. No rigid rule can be made which will apply to all, unless we wish to produce what we see in the Church of Rome, external obedience to prescribed forms, coupled with very slight manifestations of spiritual life.

The Committee of the Church Missionary Society, conscious of the importance of having in every heathen country a well-organized, independent, and self-supporting native church, has in Sierra Leone, as elsewhere, encouraged the ordination of native pastors, and the appointment of native schoolmasters. The native church of Sierra Leone now exists and flourishes. It is not, as it was some years ago, a church leaning for support on the Church of England, but it stands now in a position of independence, maintained almost entirely by its own members. The native pastorate fund receives some assistance from the Government, but relies mainly on contributions from its own church members.

The Sierra Leone Church occupies, in fact, in relation to the Church Missionary Society, the same position which a child does, who, having arrived at mature years, leaves home, and no longer lives on the resources of his parents, but maintains himself by honest industry. Yet, in the case of such a child, the old home is not forgotten, nor is his affection for those who cherished him in his infancy weakened. There can be little doubt that the Sierra Leone Church will never forget the parental care of the Church Missionary Society, and will always endeavour to acknowledge the obligation, by keeping up friendly intercourse with such missionaries of the Society as may still linger on her shores.

As for the Society itself, it can never cease to regard the Native Church of Sierra Leone with feelings similar to those entertained by parents towards a child, who, at a distance from them, occupies a new home, and has become the centre of a new circle, rejoicing in the tidings of his prosperity, and mourning with him in adversity.

The Sierra Leone Native Pastorate Auxiliary has now been in existence twelve years. Before the establishment of this auxiliary, every important post in the church of the colony was filled by an European clergyman. Now, many of those posts are filled by Africans; and Sir Benjamin Pyne, one of the Governors of the colony, in one of his letters to the Secretary of State, says:—"The clergymen belonging to this Society are, as a whole, a well-educated body of men, and well adapted to their peculiar vocation. Some of them are possessed of talents and learning which would command respect, even in the church at home."

It is no less remarkable, than strictly true, that the Sierra Leone Native Church is actuated by a deep and abiding missionary spirit. Not satisfied with ministering to their flocks, like the pastors of a Christian country in Europe, the African clergy are full of zeal for the conversion of their still heathen countrymen, and African laymen contribute liberally towards the funds required for the maintenance of missionary work. And it is worthy of notice, that the liberality of African Christians for the furtherance of missions has increased greatly since the church became independent. Whilst the church received a large amount of aid from the Church Missionary Society, its contribution towards the expenses of missions rarely, if ever, reached the sum of £100 annually. Now that it has become nearly self-supporting, and pays its own clergy about £700 a year, it contributes, on an average, £300 a year to the mission fund, besides sending help to the Bible Society, and aiding several local benevolent associations. So that, in the very spirit of the Macedonian churches of old, these West African Christians have first given themselves unto the Lord, and then abounded "unto the riches of their liberality."

There are three still unchristianized countries adjoining Sierra Leone, for which the native church has consented to provide and maintain missionaries.

The mission in the northern part of the *Quiah* country has been for the last ten years under the charge of the Rev. C. Knödler, who has learned the Timneh language. On the 18th of May, 1872, he baptized seven adults, who may be regarded as the first fruits of his mission. The southern part of the same country is under the charge of an African, the Rev. J. C. Taylor, formerly of the

Niger mission. The population is of four kinds: emigrants from Sierra Leone, Mendis, Timnehs, and Lokkos. The condition of many of the Sierra Leone settlers is very melancholy, and sometimes quite disheartening. Gross immorality, and almost total neglect of religion, exist to a great extent among them. The Mendis are more hopeful in character, although most of them are still heathen. At one place they have built for themselves a church for Christian worship capable of accommodating 200 persons. The Lokkos, on the other hand, are extremely degraded, and avoid the missionary as much as possible. The Timnehs are few in number, and intermediate in character between the Mendis and the Lokkos.

The *Sherbro* country was for several years occupied by a native schoolmaster and catechist, receiving only an occasional visit from some Sierra Leone missionary. Now, however, the mission is placed under the charge of an African, the Rev. Henry Johnson, a man of eminent ability and of fervent zeal. He has preached regularly in the numerous country villages of his district, and has often had both Mahommedans and heathens listening with the utmost attention to the truths of the gospel of the Lord Jesus Christ. His chief employment, however, has been the translation of the Scriptures into the Mendi language.

The *Bullom* country is partly under British Government and partly under that of native Mohammedan chiefs. It was long ago occupied by the missionaries of the Church Missionary Society, but it was abandoned for want of sufficient men, and there were then no native pastors to take the places left vacant by Europeans. In the year 1861, however, Mr. Boston, an African catechist, was sent there. After labouring there with great zeal and perseverance for three years, he was ordained on Trinity Sunday, 1864. He at once began to preach in the Timneh language. In 1872 he had on his list 528 church members, of whom 158 were communicants. Amongst these he reports "a growth of practical Christianity." But he, like many of his brethren, has to lament the prevalence of vice and the neglect of religion amongst many settlers from Sierra Leone.

Slowly, then, but surely the gospel is making its way amongst the tribes who live in the immediate neighbourhood of the colony; and the messengers who proclaim the "glad tidings of great joy" are no longer Europeans, but Africans.

The Chief Justice of Sierra Leone, in a letter to the local secretary of the Church Missionary Society, referring to the day of prayer which was observed in 1872 throughout the British Empire, expresses a hope that "West Africa will not be wanting in zealous and efficient men to enter into the field now being opened up by Dr. Livingstone."

An African clergyman, the Rev. G. Nicol, has lately been appointed to the chaplaincy of the Gambia; and thus another proof has been added to those already given, that Africans are capable of discharging any of the duties, and assuming any of the responsibilities which usually devolve on Europeans, provided that they receive the same intellectual training.

Undoubtedly, many of the African races, and those especially which inhabit the western portion of the continent, are steeped in barbarism; but experience does not show that greater obstacles are offered to proper training by their mental faculties than by those of any other race which has dwelt for centuries in ignorance and vice. There is every reason to believe, if we may credit the records of modern history, that the barbarism of the aborigines of Europe was far greater than that of the African of the nineteenth century: and, indeed, there are many African tribes as yet beyond the pale of humanizing influences who can boast of a higher standard of civilization than had been attained by the inhabitants of Britain before the Roman invasion.

It is really very hard to understand why the African should have been singled out for the outpourings of prejudice and ignorance. Those who have lived amongst Africans say that there can be no reason to doubt their capacity for improvement. They possess remarkable powers of observation. Their faculties of memory and mental calculation are amazing. Under favourable conditions, and with wholesome stimulus, they are active, industrious, and quick to learn. At Sierra Leone any one may any day see men who have been liberated from the hold of a slave ship, holding important public offices, taking part in the government of the colony of which they are citizens, and supporting philanthropic schemes intended to benefit their less fortunate countrymen.

Mr. Nichol at the Gambia more than realizes the expectations that were formed of him when he was appointed. His post is one of great importance and of great difficulty. He stands, as he says himself, "alone in spiritual matters; no brother pastor to consult or exchange ideas with."

"You can hardly understand," he says again, "the difficulties that lie at the threshold of the moral and social improvement of this settlement. Conceive a half-neglected, half-civilized, half-christianized community, and you have the fiction of the Gambia."

Mr. Nichol has, however, proved himself equal to cope with the difficulties which surround him. The vigour and the zeal which he has hitherto displayed are an earnest of what he is yet likely to do, if his life be spared, in promoting the spread of the gospel in the district watered by the Gambia.

I have already said that Bishop Beccles, after spending nine years in Sierra Leone, returned to England. His successor, Dr. Cheetham, who had been for some years before his elevation to the bishopric, perpetual curate of Quarndon, near Derby, arrived at Freetown on the 6th of January, 1871.

Early in the following November the Bishop held his first visitation and ordination in Sierra Leone, after which followed a Conference which lasted two days. This Conference seems to have created considerable interest, and to have given very great satisfaction. About a hundred persons attended every morning, and three times that number assembled at the evening meetings. Almost immediately after, Bishop Cheetham started for Cape Coast and Lagos. We have seen how two of his predecessors were cut down by the African fever. He, too, on his arrival at Lagos, was attacked by that enemy to the white man; but by the good providence of God his life was spared, and on the 30th of November he was able to confirm 220 English-speaking candidates at Christchurch, and a few days later a considerable number of Yoruba-speaking candidates at the Bread-fruit church.

On Advent Sunday, which intervened between the two confirmation days, the Bishop ordained four Africans named T. B. Wright, S. Pearse, D. Olubi, and D. Williams. The first of these, Mr. Wright, had been employed as a catechist in Lagos and its outskirts. Mr. Samuel Pearse had been for eleven years at Badagry, labouring under circumstances of great difficulty amongst the Popos. The other two, Mr. David Williams and Mr. Daniel Olubi, belonged to the Abbeokuta mission. The latter had at Kudete a station in the town of Ibadan a native Christian flock which then numbered 223 souls.

The six weeks spent by the Bishop at Lagos proved a season of great refreshment, not only to the missionary brethren, but to many other Christians.

On the 31st of December, 1871, the Bishop left Lagos and reached Freetown in the middle of January, 1872, rather stronger than when he left. Mrs. Cheetham, however, was suffering from the effects of the climate, and after lingering till the 23rd of May she died, adding one more illustrious name to the lost list of England's daughters who have fallen in the attempt to christianize the women of Africa.

The Bishop immediately after her death, feeling the necessity of rest and change of air, returned for a short time to England, pleaded most effectually the cause of his diocese, and went back to Sierra Leone in December, 1872.

Reviewing his labours in the month of March, 1873, the Church Missionary Record says:—" The advent of Bishop Cheetham has been of unmixed advantage to the cause of true religion."

In his charge delivered in St. George's Cathedral, Freetown, on the 24th of October, 1871, Bishop Cheetham states that there were then in the Sierra Leone division of the diocese, five European and twenty native clergymen, whose labours are assisted by fifteen native catechists, two scripture readers, and forty schoolmasters. He also says that the average attendance at the Sunday morning services in all the churches of the colony was 6480, at the Sunday evening services 5272, and on week days 987. The whole number of church members he reckons at 14,528, of whom 4215 were communicants.

What is, moreover, of immense importance, the Sierra Leone Church maintained forty-four day-schools, and thirty-two Sunday schools. In the day-schools were 3852 children, with an average attendance of 2625. In the Sunday schools were 1943 persons, many of whom were adults, and the average attendance was 1448. In conducting those Sunday schools, the clergy had the voluntary assistance of more than one hundred teachers.

After recording these facts and figures, Bishop

Cheetham adds:—" Granted that Africa, especially this West Coast, is the land of disappointment, that the history of Governments here is little else than a record of benevolent conceptions, almost entirely frustrated by providential disasters; that the history of missions is a most heart-rending tribute to an indomitable faith, hoping against hope, through 'seeing him who is invisible.' Take this statement, contrast the present with the past, and I venture to ask, has not God been faithful to his promises? May not those who have sown in tears reap in joy? Has not philanthropy, notwithstanding all its toils, reaped a great reward? Have not the men of faith who planted here the standard of the Cross reaped even beyond a reasonable expectation? What would Granville Sharp and Robert Clarkson, what would William Wilberforce and Sir Fowell Buxton say—names ever to be cherished in our midst—could they behold the things our eyes behold? How would Scott and Venn, how would Pratt and Bickersteth, acknowledge that He is faithful who hath promised. Surely here the bitterness of death is past; surely here the curse of Ham is being exchanged for the blessing of Abraham; surely the wilderness is becoming a watered garden which the Lord hath blessed."

To these encouraging words may well be added the words of Bishop Bowen, spoken in the course of a charge which he delivered in 1858:—"When we witness," he said, "the crowded congregations in the mission churches; when we see the people kneeling universally in prayer; hear the almost too loud response from nearly every lip; and then the warmth and heartiness of the song of praise; and again, meet so many—two-thirds, or sometimes three-fourths of the adults crowding to the table of our Lord, many with the marks of former heathenism in their faces; what Christian, I ask, but would thank God for these things, and would see in these great results the value of missionary labours in general, and would acknowledge the unmistakable mark of Divine approbation on the efforts and scriptural principles of that great Society which has been such an honoured instrument in the hands of God for planting the Church of Christ on these shores."

I have sketched briefly, but as accurately as I possibly could, the Missionary History of Sierra Leone; and have traced the course of events in which the Church Missionary Society was concerned in that colony, from the year 1816 to the present time.

Whatever may be said or thought of missionary work in general, none but those who wilfully close their eyes to shut out the light of truth, will be disposed to deny that in Sierra Leone at least, it has proved eminently successful, and has achieved wonderful results. There, at any rate, the gospel has asserted its Divine origin and its irresistible power, and has triumphed over obstacles which might have been thought insuperable. Sierra Leone Pagan and Sierra Leone Christian form a contrast which must fill every beholder with amazement; and compel even from unwilling lips the declaration :—" Thou art great and doest wondrous things ; thou art God alone." Let it never be said after what it has pleased God to do in Sierra Leone by the instruments whom He has raised up, that the gospel of the Lord Jesus Christ has in this nineteenth century lost any of its vitality ; and that the labour of love and the prayer of faith will ever prove altogether fruitless. Rather let every true-hearted missionary as he goes forth to toil, perhaps to die, in the service of his Divine Master, be encouraged by the words of the greatest missionary that the world ever saw :—" Be ye steadfast, unmoveable, always abounding in the work of the Lord, for as much as ye know that *your labour is not in vain* in the Lord."

To those—and they are many—who unhappily care not for the spiritual results of missionary work, I say that that work, even on the low ground of worldly policy, has a claim on the sympathy of every one within whose bosom beats a human heart.

Wherever missionary work succeeds, there many mere worldly blessings follow in its train. One fact in the history of Sierra Leone proves this beyond all dispute.

On the 10th of October, 1860, His Royal Highness Prince Alfred—the Duke of Edinburgh—visited Freetown and received an enthusiastic welcome from all classes of the community. He was met on the wharf by the Governor, the Members of Council, the Clergy—twelve of whom were Africans —the Officers of the Garrison, the Merchants and other gentlemen, some of whom presented addresses. The whole way from the wharf to the Government House was lined with the children of the various schools, who, to the number of a thousand, dressed in white, occupied each side of the way, and sang as His Royal Highness passed along, the National Anthem. Amongst other addresses, one was presented from twenty-three gentlemen representing the liberated Africans of the colony and their descendants. In that document the following words occur:—" We cannot refrain from pointing Your Royal Highness to the thousands of free men who hail with acclamations of delight your advent among us. Think of them hunted, beaten, branded, degraded below the beasts of the field, by a slavery ending but with death. Compare that picture to this which presents itself to the contemplation of Your Royal Highness to-day. Behold a population whose very bearing proclaims their freedom to the world, surrounded with all the elements of an advancing civilization, and enjoying a widely-spreading Christianity? Our hearts beat high with hope that the impressions which the mind of Your Royal Highness shall have received during your present visit, will convince you that *England has not laboured for the amelioration of our race in vain.*"

The missionary works for time and for eternity; for neither does he labour *in vain*.

The man of the world will look at the secular blessings which closely follow his footsteps: the faithful Christian will prefer to look at the great spiritual results which, with the Divine assistance, accompany his exertions.

The civilization and the worldly prosperity which accompany the diffusion of the religion of Christ may be seen now, and when seen, may easily be appreciated at their full value: but the spiritual results of the work done by faithful missionaries in every part of the world will not be realized until the day on which that sublime prophecy shall be fulfilled:—"After this I beheld, and lo! a great multitude which no man could number, *of all nations, and kindreds, and people, and tongues*, stood before the throne and before the Lamb clothed with white robes and palms in their hands: And cried with a loud voice saying, Salvation to our God which sitteth upon the throne and unto the Lamb. And all the angels stood round about the throne and about the elders and the four beasts (or living ones) and fell before the throne on their faces and worshipped God; saying Amen; Blessing, and glory, and wisdom, and thanksgiving, and honour, and power, and might be unto our God for ever and ever. Amen."

www.ingramcontent.com/pod-product-compliance
Lightning Source LLC
Chambersburg PA
CBHW021402230426
43666CB00006B/613